SILENT BIRTHS:
FRUIT OF THE WOMB

By

Elaine Cordani-Gelhaus

ISBN: 1-4033-0902-7 (Softcover)
ISBN: 1-4033-3577-X (Hardcover)

This book is printed on acid free paper.

1stBooks – rev. 06/13/02

To contact Elaine Cordani-Gelhaus –
re seminars/workshops/book purchase
Email Address: CORDANIGELHAUS@AOL.COM

TABLE OF CONTENTS

CHAPTER   TITLE   PAGE

PART ONE: "PAIN AND SUFFERING"

I.   "COMMUNION" 1
II.   "HERSTORY/HISTORY" 5
III.   "TO EVERY TIME THERE IS A SEASON: 9
IV.   "THE MIRACLE" 15
V.   "CAPE COD AND BEYOND" 18
VI.   "MYSTERY" 24
VII.   "FAMILY" 29
VIII.   "COMING HOME - THE VISION" 34
IX.   "LINEAGE" 40
X.   "HANDS RECLAIMED" 46
XI.   "THE LINEAGE DEEPENS" 53
XII.   "LOSS OF INNOCENCE" 56
XIII.   "DEATH NOT QUITE YET" 60
XIV.   "THE BURIAL" 65

PART TWO: "REDEMPTION AND RESURRECTION

XV.   "LIFE" 72
XVI.   "MOTHER'S DAY" 77
XVII.   "BODYWORK AND OLD TEARS" 82
XVIII.   "BODYWORK & MOTHER" 84
XIX.   "MOTHER" 86
XX.   "NEW HOMES" 90
XXI.   "LEAVING HOME" 102
XXII.   "LOVE'S TEST" 104
XXIII.   "PONDERING THE MEANING OF THINGS" 109
XXIV.   "TURNING POINT TO NEW BEGINNINGS" 117
XXV.   "HALF-PACKED AND READY TO GO!" 120
XXVI.   "HOUSECLEANING" 122
XXVII.   "LILACS, DEAD ROOTS AND ROSES" 127
XXVIII.   "THE BABY IN THE BUTTON BOX" 134

CONSECRATION

To the Divine Mother in gratitude and deep love.
To My Mother as I honor and bear witness to her silent
And ever painful births.
To the Divine Feminine Presence in all of us.

To past, present and future generations
Of my Lineage. Godspeed.

To the Silent, Nameless, Voiceless Births and Ghosts of the past.
I send you love and wishes for healing.

To my Beloved Children and my Father
Who I pray will understand the value of
Claiming one's voice.
And come to know me for not only
The Mother that I am
But the woman I have become.

To my Beloved Brother
Who has supported me every step of my way.
God Bless you.

To my Husband and our life as a family.
To my Lover, who taught me
Unconditional Love,
Especially for myself.

To the Shaman, Pharaoh and Swami.
I owe you thanks for rising from the Phoenix's ashes!

PROLOGUE

I invite you to question your reality, and be forewarned, for the following events will challenge them. This is but one example of what lies within and beyond our presently held world view. You'll be surprised beyond belief! For you will not only read, but energetically experience with these words, my true life phenomena open to all who dare to forge new roads. I offer the reader who is fearless enough to do so, to be open to trust and just be in your individual experience. The following opportunity to heal in a most unusual and heart rending manner will be yours, to keep for your lifetimes.

My mother came to me from beyond the illusory veil of the beyond, where death takes one to be transformed to eternal life, seeking redemption and forgiveness; haunted by ghosts of past deeds. Her last gift of love was fueled by the fires of her passion, pain and shame. It is also humanities story of love, betrayal and torment producing soul sickness that subsequently affects heart, mind and body. It is a story of past deeds, of illegitimate children, abortions, darkness haunting the daylight of the present. It is a story of a mother whose life had meaning beyond the agony of her intense suffering

I hope that others may understand not only her deeds, but yours as well, and through understanding and acceptance, you will not only know myself and my mother, but women in bodies of roles society puts upon us. Then, and only then, will we be able to make peace - within ourselves, others and throughout this temporary sacred space we live in - called Mother Earth.

As a young child and woman, mystical experiences heightened. Unbeknownst to me, my relationship with my parents was just what my soul needed to recover the lost hope of my beloved mother. It also involved my relationship with my husband when a bloodstain appeared on my white blouse, only to suddenly disappear, with my aunt as a witness of this phenomena. After that event, I revisited the question I initially had before I married - "What Is Love?" It furthered my life purpose in those and succeeding relationships, to be relived in the present, from past lives clamoring for healing.

For the past 18 years, I've worked in the "shadow" society of mental illness, psychosis, addictions with its' gripping behaviors, as well as with developmentally disabled, whom I dearly loved, and on to working in community and private practice serving scores of individuals and couples who wished to move beyond their grief to joy in finding lost parts of themselves.

Spirituality came easy to me. However, it was a hard sell to others. I became healer of the mind, embodiment of the soul, integrating spirit and matter through conventional and unconventional realms of psychic phenomena. My work with others as well as my personal journey intensified. I counsel clients in traveling and experiencing fields of paranormal consciousness, guiding them in this much misunderstood world of God's wonders.

My experience working in psychiatry saw spirituality manifest in aberrant forms, but nonetheless, related to God. Indeed, I found there is a fine line between psychosis and spirituality. One is rewarded for the latter, and punished for the former. However, they're only different roads to the same place - Home! Passion's ignition led to an out-patient substance abuse unit and the Twelve Steps, where "God" was not a dirty word. I found that God invariably comes in the "Back Doors" of life, when one is vulnerable and open. I creatively used God's out-of-fashion ways in my work as a therapist, where I studied aspects of self and personality, and helped people integrate psychotherapy with spirituality with application of The Twelve Steps.

So God was in fashion in addictions, mental illnesses and psychosis. However, mental illness was seldom addressed in the so-called "normal" world of neurosis. I soon discovered one had to have a "label" in order to know oneself, but I chose to pursue those discoveries without judgment of people. My conviction was that "soul sickness" leads people to act out in many forms but really the question that needed to be answered again, was "What is my life purpose?" - and to seek the answer from the Source!

This ever deepening levels of discovery, wonder, and awe at God's mysterious Universe was different, somewhat frightening at first, but, indeed that is the way of Spirit. In my journey to essence, and only when I was unconsciously ready, a Shaman came to me, whom I intensely trained with for several years. One of my experiences was to actually _see_ steam emanating out of my finger from excess energy, as we worked on the phone with a visualization exercise. This is but one example of my experience with our Human Energy System. I became a Transformer of Spiritual Energy, where I had visions, telepathy, and channeling. In one group session, I **_became_** the deceased, feeling that soul's emotions, and helped heal a long-standing unresolved relationship with one of the persons attending the group.

Past lives weren't one of my priorities, but one that cropped up on the road of what I call "Divine Order and Purpose." Apparently I was ready. Only I didn't consciously know that, but my soul did. In my training as a channeler, I was put in touch with a person who had enormous healing abilities. A former Pharaoh came to me, a friend from a past life. Later on, my friend on his travels to Egypt, was informed that I was Queen Hatshepsut from the Third Century, and gifted with an actual piece of the Pyramid, a tuning fork, and the finest frankincense and myrrh. I have yet to meet this "stranger" from my present life. But look at the wonder and marvel of the gifts presented by living Life's Mysteries.

I was stunned, for like many other "normal"people, felt I had all to do with resolution of current relationships, which seemed more than enough for many life times. My shamanic training, channeling and mentoring by my new/old friend, encompassed 119 days of spiritual testing. It is at that point, in an email one day from him, that I was informed, as well, of my past former Pharaoh status. My spiritual testing intensified.

Mysterious events happened in a ritual of discovery of other past lives. During one, I was telepathically visited by His Holiness, the Dalai Lama. If was as real as if I were carrying on a phone conversation with one of my friends. I was tired at the time, and the Blessed Mother came to me saying "You missed the message." "What message?" I replied, and later "waking" up to yet another astounding event realized what had occurred. His Holiness came to me three times, during and after a past life purification ritual wherein I saw 30 of my past lives in a mirror.

My circuitous path took many turns, with seemingly dead ends. I soon found out that the Soul is relentless in pursuit of excellence, whether one liked it or not, one was forever being prodded onward and upward. Another person entered, my lover, bearing another piece of my former and present life's puzzle. There were remnants from a past life that needed to be healed as well. All the pieces of God's and my tapestry were now coming together in discovering and recovering my former lifetimes' mystical qualities, to be integrated and made whole with my present life. It is like going up into an attic and opening up old and dusty "treasure" chest of the past, that act like a circuitous DNA with a cast of characters that confront each soul's journey.

To highlight silent ghosts of past deeds, and my contract with God, I had unknowingly carried the dead energy of painful and lost births from my mother's womb till only recently. This was confirmed with, and seen by another wise sage, a Himalayan Swami. It is she that you will read about in this book as well. A young woman I had known for one week ten years ago, to suddenly come to my home this past summer to do intense work from my life as a Pharaoh as well as present issues with family members. I truly believe she was sent to me by God.

This autobiographical story goes back in time, ten years ago. The search for meaning ended with the beginning of this book. And so, here we are in the present - a journey started with one question and bewilderment that continues to surpass my wildest dreams. And so it is, for now. In a sense there is no ending to this book. For once one lives the true mystery of life, Life then mirrors the unfolding and ever infinite universe. This is just one chapter.

Come join me in my soul journey. Perhaps you will recognize part of your soul's calling to find your yearnings come to fruition in embodying your life story. It is my fervent wish that you do. Indeed, we are here not only to suffer, but to ascend to our essence from the pain and sorrow. This is the true meaning of life, the alchemy of transformation open to all.

CHAPTER ONE: "COMMUNION"

I focused in the moment. There was chant music playing. For some unknown, but perfectly natural reason, my mouth began to move as if I were silently speaking to someone. Neither hearing a reply or actually mouthing any words, I began to sob, knowing, sensing, the importance of the moment. "Where are you?" I said, the words finally uttered. They were directed to my recently deceased mother.

I closed my eyes and saw a vision of her as a young woman. She was smiling the same smile in the picture in my parents' home, only this time she wasn't in a photograph, but visiting me as I was receiving healing energy work from Madeline. She looked beautiful; her wide, round, dark brown eyes shining, her mouth stretched in a joyful smile. I took note of her graceful long nose, and curly hair ringing her face. My mind battled with this strange reality. I closed my eyes, shook my head as if this weren't happening. But it was happening! I yearned for some confirmation from Madeline, but didn't want to interrupt her work. Then, quite playfully, opened one eye and winking, said "Is that you, Mom?" Her swift reply, "Yes, it's me!" I sobbed with tears of quiet gratitude.

We began a forty-five minute silent dialogue that was disturbed by my logical, and rational mind. At times, I would again shake my head trying to pry loose this strange reality; yet knowing full well and quite consciously that "Yes, my deceased mother is really speaking to me."

I already knew that today would be a special day, rushing out the front door with my bagel in hand. I had called Madeline, my healing bodywork practitioner that morning, asking for an earlier appointment. "You read my mind, Elaine. I just had a cancellation and was going to call you!" In no time at all I was in her tiny, sun and energy-filled cottage that I felt so at home in.

I excitedly described my experiences since last we met. I told her how I had dreaded the first anniversary of my mother's death, and how, the day before, I felt I was sent to a specific shop in nearby Piermont. Piermont is a small river town in Rockland County. It recently was gentrified after Woody Allen filmed many movies there. One can see the Tappan Zee Bridge off in the distance. I liked wandering in the small shops weekdays when it's quiet, especially Mairead's store. Today was just that day. I drove slowly along the river road past large Victorian homes, fantasizing that one day I would live by the river. It was part of my daily routine, adopted since an accident forced me to give up my psychotherapy practice. Today was a beautiful sunny day with the sun glistening like tiny diamonds on the Hudson River. Sailboats were bobbing along with the rhythm of the water, cheerfully greeting the warm Spring day. Once there, the store owner, Maggie, and I chatted as I looked around the store. She had a variety of interesting items from all corners of the world. While we were speaking, I noticed a small statue of the Blessed Mother that was directly in front of me on her desk. My consciousness immediately took note. Something felt strange but I couldn't identify it, as yet.

Since I was a young child, I felt drawn to Her. As I matured, I realized that the Virgin personifies archetypal symbology representing love, hope and strength. I connected with her at an early age, necessarily searching in my spiritual world for some port in a storm from painful life experiences.

A phone call came just as Maggie was speaking of the rosary beads that sold out as fast as they arrived in her store. "Look, Elaine, see Her image," as she held the crucifix up to the light for me. There in the tiny magnifying glass was an image of the Virgin. Continuing with her phone conversation, she handed the rosary beads to me. "Would you like to have these? I can't sell them, for they're imperfect." I was stunned and accepted them humbly as she easily continued with her phone conversation. I held them gently and profoundly. My brain was whirring, sensing something important about to happen. The momentum was quickening. I knew this was another of the marvelous gifts I had recently, and unexpectedly, received from yet another store owner. I sensed there was another message of love here, for myself, as well as for Mairead.

We chatted for several minutes more before I left. The rosary beads firmly gripped in my hand, almost as if I were clutching them for strength in this sacred moment. Once outside, I sobbed, knowing I was again touched by Mary and my mother. Only after mass the next day did the full realization dawn. Mairead is a Gaelic name for

Margaret! Margaret! My mother's name! I had received yet another communication from the otherworld!

I also spoke to Madeline about the strange occurrence early Easter Sunday morning. At 2:30am, no longer able to sleep, I cried out to God asking "WHAT is my life's purpose?" The question came after a sustained period of unknowingness. I had intuitively given up my practice out of intense physical pain after an accident that injured my entire spinal column. That was a year ago and I still didn't know "where I was going." Since then, I had been relying on faith and inner guidance as sustenance in the void of new beginnings, as well as healing on the outer. I insisted on answers right away instead of enjoying the journey, safe in Faith's arms, but not an easy task, especially in our hectic, fearful world.

I no sooner asked the question, when I received a vision of Jesus's head encircled with the Crown of Thorns; the same Crown of Thorns I had held in a procession in church as a young, innocent Italian Catholic female. My journal indicates that while receiving this message, I saw the image of a white dove, a symbol of the Holy Spirit. In addition, the word "History" came to me…"History?" I was puzzled. Then a vision of a hand. And then "Eggs" and "Herstory." Recognition came in the form of an outpouring of tears, tears of knowing the magnitude of what had occurred. "His story." "Her story." "Write." Tears flowed down my face. Tears of sadness for my parents' silent pain. Tears of joy for myself. I was heard! My intuition and vision of writing was to become reality. I was now able to surrender to a peaceful sleep, comforted by God's loving presence.

Madeline was listening intently as I added "Oh, yes, I almost forgot! There was a strange dream, something about the Blessed Mother and Communion." I had continued to speak and think about that dream all week. It lingered all week in my consciousness." I knew it was important but didn't find out until later how important and prophetic it was to be.

"I dreamt I was by a side altar at my childhood parish church, St. Dominic's in the Bronx. The dream was about food and the Blessed Mother. I wanted some food. Finally, after going from place to place, I wound up in a stadium. It was crowded with people. In the center, was a huge decorated, creamy white cake. I was on the ground level, the same level as the statue of Mary. I went directly to

3

it. However, when I got to Her, the statue was taken up into the crowd. I was angry. I had missed her. The ceremony was a Communion ceremony."

I stopped talking to Madeline, conscious of not wanting to take more of our precious time together with words, and anxious for the energy work to begin. I let the meaning of the dream go and continued with preparation for our work together. We were now ready to start the second phase of healing bodywork. Madeline smiled and we joked about never knowing what would happen once I got on the table. We both were quiet, concentrating on the inner. I eagerly hopped onto the massage table and closed my eyes. Madeline said she was going to lower the heat first. While she was talking I immediately began to experience new and strange sensations. There was a strong, magnetic-like pull on my head. I felt as if Madeline were going further and further away, her voice seemingly receding into the far distance. I called out to her "Where are you?" "Why, Elaine, here I am!" I was shocked to see her at my feet! How could that be for I felt she was still behind me by my head? Something very strange was happening. Time suddenly entered a strange time warp. Though puzzled I continued in this state, quieted down and remained alert and open.

"What is going on at my head?" It was a very odd sensation. I decided to find out by breathing into the sensation and trying to relax. What occurred was incredible. My mouth began to move though I uttered not a word. Some part of me understood that I was having a silent conversation. But with whom? I repeated out loud "Where are you?" calling forth the unseen person. No sooner had I closed my eyes, that my mother's face appeared to me in a vision! The rest is history, or, should I say herstory!

CHAPTER TWO: "HERSTORY/HISTORY"

"4/9/97: My mother's eyes. What secrets do they hold? I will never know them for she is forever gone. I need only make some sense for myself out of life. I believe she had a happy childhood before her parents died. Afterwards, I'm not so sure."

The above few sentences were written the day before I went to Madeline's. It was written quite spontaneously. I jotted it down in a separate, new part of my journal entitled "Creative Thoughts." I thought it strange at the time but my life, since the accident, was anything but normal! I am learning that "strange" IS "normal" and just go along with it for it has taken me to many wonderful places.

Today is one of them and a cause for much celebration and rejoicing. Filled with overflowing love, passion and joy in my heart, I added the following to the journal, knowing that the "Thought" is now a "Creation":

"4/10/97: I am sitting in FDR State Park in Peekskill, NY. I have just come from Madeline and bodywork. The day is sunny. There's a brook to my right. In front of me is the entrance to the park; now quiet before the onslaught of summer pedestrians. I came here because of this extraordinary day. It started out quite ordinary; though in thinking back, the signs were there just waiting to be connected. And were they…three and perhaps more generations' worth!"

"Two world's converging. Two generations re-emerging. I am in this world, but not of this world. To my right the brook gurgles, as birds happily chirp as spring re-emerges. A runner comes by. A truck bounces swiftly past me. Are people aware of their Life Drama? Some yes, others no, and many unfortunately may die that way."

I am wearing history and herstory on my body–my engagement ring from a past marriage; a bracelet once lost. An identical one given to my youngest daughter and later returned to me when I lost mine. My step-grandmother's diamond earrings, inherited from my mother.

And today, and the many pages, memories and feelings to come, will I speak of her life story and mine. The lineage continues strengthened by this timely and deeply mystical connection with my mother through this incredible "Communion" experience. Truly, this book is born from this wonderful creation. A creation born out of the ashes of the painful seeds of two generations' suffering, till finally coming alive and giving birth - through decay, through dead and dying bodies, through a lifetime of pain and despair - to hope, freedom and redemption. For my mother's life, as all our lives, are not lived, or suffered in vain. Finally, the process of alchemy comes alive — through forgiveness, to Love!

Slowly the ordinary merged into the extraordinary. Years, tears and a century has passed before this book could be birthed. Somehow I knew I was to write many years ago, but it took my mother's recent visit from beyond the veil and illusion of death, her several abortions, an illegitimate sister, as well as my mother's death, for it's conception.

I now have permission to speak, to tell her story and, in so doing, speak of our heritage so that not only I may be freed but my deceased mother as well. For her life had meaning. And so the "herstory" will now become "history" and give rise and birth to a redemptive memory no longer embodied in mystery, shame and guilt. For today I received in bodywork the Holy Spirit in the form of the Holy Sacrament to give voice to and proclaim my family's redemptive qualities, from seemingly endless pain and suffering, and a validation to set forth and free the secret that gripped, and perhaps crippled, our lineage for many generations. In the process of attempting to find my sister, I'm finding my roots as well as charting new territories for future generations. This is my deepest hope for my beloved children and my grandchildren. To bring hope alive again, the hope that my mother lost many times over in her lifetime.

The dialogue with my deceased mother continued. At times, I would shake my head trying to loosen this strange reality; yet knowing full well and quite consciously that "Yes, this is really happening." I cried out "Yes, I understand," not consciously knowing what I understood but rather sensing it. I asked Madeline for feedback for at that point I needed some grounding of this unreality with another. She acknowledged that it was my mother, as well as many other beings in the room including the Blessed Mother. At one level, my mother told Madeline to have me breathe deeper. Indeed, in earlier conversations with Madeline, I had been informed that it is difficult for beings to contact us on Earth, because of the density and lower vibrations here. Funny, isn't it, when we call a person "dense?" Laughing and sobbing with joy, I tried to do so.

Once my feelings and experiences were confirmed, I again sobbed in exquisite joy that my mother was here talking to and with me! She asked me to write a book about "Herstory." As usual, patterns from our former "earthly relationship" emerged. I retorted "But what about Dad? Is it to be about the family?" "No, it's to be my story!" I pressed on. This time the adolescent part said "What if I don't want to do it!" At that point, the silent room erupted with harsh, banging sounds, though Madeline and I were the only ones in the house. I got the message! Just do it!

I received more information. "It's to be about the baby." Huh? "Your mother's unborn baby that died with Grandma when she fell off the back porch?" "Yes." OK, now I get it. But there was more. I supposed at that point it was a mother-daughter thing. My mind scrambled to make some sense out of this. It was searching for one of the "mailboxes" we have in our memory bank. There was none. This required a new paradigm, a new 'mailbox.' "What am I to write about?" "I will be told."

I didn't think my mind could hold any more incredulous news but it had to for I was told…"about the baby that died before you, so you could write this book." I was in shock, sobbing profusely. I had always known my mother had several abortions. She would speak of them when in crisis with one of her many illnesses. My mother then said "You have a sister living in New Jersey." The sobbing intensified to a crescendo. This confirmed my suspicions, when, as a youngster, I found a picture of a newborn in the cedar chest. My mother had rebuked me when I showed it to her and asked "Whose baby is this?" Now, however, it felt like vilification and validation at the same time. It was so immense that I couldn't comprehend its enormity until months later. The last message from my mother…"Oh, yes, and buy a new book to write in." I smiled "Yes, Mom."

Madeline's process was just as incredible. She questioned her "guides" about the meaning of my receiving Holy Communion from many beings, first Mary and then others. The response: "we are all connected." I now understood what the dream meant. It is a portent of the future. It was my REBIRTH! That ceremony was the start of my new life, one that I had hoped and prayed for since the accident.

Madeline also received the word "alchemy" which sums up my mother's life. I had now birthed not a silent birth, but a joyous birth, a new creation with my mother. Her life's purpose and mine were now exquisitely clear. There are no accidents!

CHAPTER THREE:

"TO EVERY TIME THERE IS A SEASON:
TO EVERY LIFE THERE IS A REASON"

The string of events that happened on the first anniversary of my mother's death, was the culmination of, and transition to, an important phase of my life. The early years that I'd spent yearning for love, questioning love, giving workshops on love, produced fertile soil for these, my later years.

My mother often referred to losing hope, but always in the context of her favorite bracelet, of faith, hope and charity charms. Little did I know the depth and significance of what she alluded to. I never asked her WHY she lost hope. I regret that now. However, my quest in life unconsciously revolved around traveling the road of hope, and of love. Unbeknownst to me at the time, I was in search of her lost, precious treasures. They were mine as well.

Since her death, change now represents a celebration of life, rather than something to be feared. I thought, "we're not separated by death! In fact, we are united in a rebirthing process, though in different dimensions." We are separate beings, not mother and daughter, but souls united in birth, souls freed in death - a healthy freedom. The bond seems strengthened by that thought.

The metaphor of a plant is aptly suited to the human experience of change. The seeds require time, time in the form of patience; tending his or her soil and soul. Once a new shoot appears, the earth's terrain, or human psyche is no longer the same. There is a new space, an opening for new life, for healthy growth.

In a similar vein, I too am like the plant. My view is uncluttered by the "dirt" around me. I am peeking anew from a deeper and more humble position, that of higher consciousness. Though at times my world felt as if it had turned upside down, I actually landed right side up! Life looks exquisitely better from this position. My experiences changed beliefs, values, and subsequently attitudes and behaviors.

I now deeply know, from experiencing life's mysteries, that there IS a Divine Plan, and most importantly, in Divine Time. For each precious life has the opportunity for rebirth. Glorious new life sprouts from the painful void, and voice, of the unknown. I had ventured

9

forth into unknown territory. Faith, in turn, gifted me with new birth. My emptiness, loneliness and courage paid off. By forging a new path, I have found a new road. And for the first time, I feel as if I'm finally living MY life, as a co-creator with God.

I'm sixty as I write this. I am now able to look back at my personal, professional and spiritual life and see connections that time has gifted me with. My yearnings have been well spent. They have given me a rich and rewarding life, especially in the past twenty years. I've mellowed to the wise, mature and beautiful woman, that I both dreamt of becoming, written about, and am now living. Life is exquisitely more interesting and defining than ever before.

The intersection of generations, of a deceased mother, and very much alive daughter— produce profoundly powerful, though silent and unconscious, cataclysmic rippling effects for my family. I have no doubt that ultimately each succeeding generation will be touched by what is happening now. I look with love, pride and honor to each vulnerable soul. After all the rage, anger and frustration towards parents, children, ex-husband, lover and especially myself, I have come to an inner acceptance and openness to "what is" rather than what "should be."

As a result, my entire being has changed. The Communion ceremony resulted in incredible energy, energy no longer internal but external. The ceremony was for the two parts of myself; the union of opposites and the final integration of spirit and matter within one's psyche. There's a redemptive quality here, for my suffering, as well as for our family's worth from seemingly endless pain, and a validation to go forth and set free the secret that silently gripped our lineage.

I write here of born and unborn children, voice and voiceless babies, and ones who gave them life as well as being claimed by death. I write for the voice, to the voiceless of past generations, so that the silence may now have a name. My mother would often shyly speak of her abortions while waiting for her doctor in the emergency room. She also voiced her pain to others of "having to give her babies away." Either given away for adoption, or cruelly shorn of two babies, suffice is to say that all their lives had meaning. My mother's pain would emanate from her stomach; the container of her life-long testimony of sorrow. Quietly, her body and mind tried to make sense of her agony. I fear it never did. She died with her secret, only to return one more time to reveal to me her truths. If ever I doubted there was a God; if ever I believed I was alone in the universe; those doubts have been pulverized by my mystical experiences. If ever I doubted there is an afterlife, and mistrusted life's process and meaning, this too has passed. The reappearance of my mother was another string of messages from the "other world." When one experiences firsthand the presence of the numinous, there is no longer doubt, but Faith...a Faith that now begins to be tested! My journey had only begun!

The journey has taken me down many a long, lonely and painful road searching for the love and hope my mother lost. I've no regrets. And as I look back, the most meaningful events came to me synchronistically.

Summer was beckoning me to Cape Cod. A beckoning to return to the sea; "Mare," "Mary," "Mother." Return to Motherhood was what I needed to get out of my slump. Perhaps a more positive word would be "slumber" - the period of dreamland in which hibernation processes give way to birth; the birth of creativity.

Pondering recent events, I sat at my desk, now newly planted in the living room of my beautiful apartment, on top of which was the recently resurrected computer. The computer had been a purchase from my lover several years ago. I remember the day with fondness, as a smile spreads brightly on my face. He had suggested, until stopped by my rigidity against things mechanical, that I "try out the computer to see how I liked it." Time passed without taking him up on his offer. Soon after we made a date to see one another. The doorbell rang. No one answered. Then I heard footsteps. Up the stairs he came, with big box in hand, and a glorious grin on his face. "I thought you might change your mind," says he. In he strode, into my office, plops the "thing from a strange, logical, rational land" onto MY desk, which MY son had recently assembled. "Here are the instructions, and you even have a key to your own box," says he with a lascivious grin.

For days the computer sat on MY desk. I would fume each time I looked at "IT" with rage. I was very aware of the reason why. I had come a long way since my innocent youth. The assertive woman in me was screaming that he was taking over MY SACRED SPACE! A

11

week went by, and then I was energized into action! "Aha, I know exactly what I will do." Soon after, the computer was "dethroned," and relegated to the realm of the shadow; the closet. Now everything would continue to be neat and tidy. "Just like the relationship," - "in the closet." When we next met, my lover would smile at my creative solution. For months and years on end, the computer would be hidden, as would our relationship.

The state of our relationship paralleled my state of mind. Indeed, my very state of being. "Such was my world!," I thought. "When would it change?" I was frustrated in all areas of my life. I needed a drastic change. Unbeknownst to me at the time, I was soon to receive my wish. But it came in an unexpected form; that of a strange and unchartered path that began several years hence.

Since my return from Cape Cod, newly found energy manifested itself in the need to change, to let go, to empty out for new growth. Deeply imbedded yearnings were to fuel the momentum that had begun after the Einstein Dream Seminar at the Cape that was part of my educational training as a clinical social worker on a psychiatric in-patient unit. A new chapter in my life was starting; a chapter that would propel me to a new plane of consciousness. It all began with a phone call. It was Barbara calling from the front desk. "Elaine, have I got a girl for you! She's lovely, Indian and delightful." Something in me knew that this was not another chance introduction. "Barbara, for God's sake, not another woman! What about a man?" "Well, there is someone single next door to you, but you'll like this woman. Besides, she hasn't a car and is here all the way from India." "India?" My ears perked up. "Barbara, I can't deal with this right now. I'll talk to you in the morning."

It was Sunday evening. I had gotten up at 5AM, and was tired from the long ride from New York. Once off the highway, I had leisurely driven the winding country roads up the Cape. I loved that route. I sighed and felt better already as I passed row upon row of neatly, and newly budding summer flowers. The colors and smells were already invigorating my spirit. I was home! I arrived at the motel, unpacked, and soon became increasingly impatient. I wanted to go to the beach. The beach in essence was my "mountain," one that I yearly returned to, taking inventory of where I had been and where I was going, both in my job as a Social Worker as well as my personal life. I quickly changed and walked to the beach just in time to see the sunset. Barbara's phone call was put on hold, but there was something about it that I sensed to be important and would deal with it later.

One of the rituals at the beach was to walk to the edge of the majestic cliffs and watch the sparkling diamond-like objects the sun made on the waves. I never tired of the sight and smells of the ocean, seagulls overhead, and giggling children with their shovels and pails eagerly digging long trenches for the water to enfold. Once I did that, I descended exactly forty-two stairs and walked away from the crowd, to a private part of the beach. I strolled along the shoreline to look for "heart-shaped" rocks. I usually found a few and would invariably give them away to special people, my lover usually being among them. He would never reply, just smiled and thanked me in his quiet way. Also, once up at the Cape, I'd think of our relationship and the mystery of it all. With unanswered questions, but filled up and fortified from my recent experiences, I returned to the motel, now ready for new adventures.

The next day, the first of five conference days, soon arrived. It was always a pleasant experience to be at the Cape, and to awaken to the sound of birds announcing another God-given day. The joy I felt soon turned to puzzlement. For upon awakening, the residue of a dream about the Blessed Mother was on my mind. I remembered the events of two years ago when I sat in a church in Mt. Vernon, NY. I thought it strange to be reminded of these events now. But how could I forget that day; the day of my miracle of the pen! I had demanded a miracle from Mary, and after three hours in church received one! "Strange to think of this now." I wondered why. I'd soon find out.

I dressed and walked the pebbled road to the main house. I loved walking on the pebbles. They made a crunchy sound that reminded me of my childhood days when I felt carefree and joyful. That was how I felt that morning, alive and excited to start the day. I turned the corner of the motel's inviting Cape Cod style house eager to see who was on the familiar patio that interested me, in addition to the donuts and coffee!

I sat down next to a handsome looking man with a beard. Beards are a turn-on for me. I associate them with intellectual "territory," which I value. I wasn't disappointed. He was an English professor with an expertise in myths. We spoke about Joseph Campbell. Soon, the conversation flowed into a highly philosophical vein. Much to my surprise and amusement, up he bounds and hurries out of sight! "Oh, well, I thought, perhaps I had better stick to finding out who this young woman is from India." Just as I said that, Leonilla turned the corner. She had wonderful, large brown eyes, was about thirty years old, dark skinned, slim, with a very pronounced demeanor. We eyed one another discreetly, neither approaching the other. I took note, but decided I wasn't yet ready to speak to her. My mind returned to the reverie of this morning's events that were very special to me. The fact of the matter was that I had received my miracle but I didn't quite know what to DO with it!

CHAPTER FOUR: "THE MIRACLE"

The year was 1990. I was invited to an event that would slowly change my life. A Catholic church in Mt. Vernon, NY, was holding an unusual prayer service. A couple from Sedona, Arizona was to speak about daily apparitions from the Blessed Mother. Flocks of devout worshipers came to their home, and it was widely publicized nationwide.

I had been invited to the church by my colleague, Bill, a male nurse on the Outpatient Substance Abuse Unit, that I "backed into" after my stint in psychiatry. "Backed into" was the term I used in my interview with the psychiatrist. I was astute enough to know that working on a substance abuse unit would entail a challenge; not with the patients, but with the staff that would parallel the behavior of the afflicted addict.

At the time I was employed as a Social Worker at a large metropolitan hospital in the Bronx. The hospital was near my parents' home. I had taken a social work position there for two reasons; one unfinished business with my parents, and the other to work in psychiatry. After three years on a psych inpatient unit, I transferred to the outpatient department, working with the teachings and valued tools of recovery; the Twelve Steps. The unit suited my psychological and spiritual interests, as well as furthering my goal of private practice.

The day on the unit is fresh in my memory. I had gone to Bill's office to thank him for the Miraculous Medal he had given me from his recent trip to Medjugore, which I kept in my pocketbook. He had some photos from there, told me about the daily miracles such as the sun turning on its axis, and spoke of people who had taken photos of the sky only to see the image of Mary once the pictures were developed. I loved hearing stories such as these, for they always fascinated and mystified me. Noting my excitement, he asked me if I'd be interested in coming to a church to hear about further testimonies about the Blessed Mother. I quickly responded, not waiting for details, "I'll be there."

It seemed that the unbelieving wife had a dream of the Blessed Mother. That morning she told her husband about it, who then painted a picture of the Virgin. The next day, the Virgin appeared from the painting, while the couple was praying the rosary. Subsequently, throngs of worshipers came to see the apparitions, leaving with wonder, awe and amazement. Mrs. Ruiz, now deeply devoted to the Blessed Mother, later appeared on two daytime tv shows, Sally Jesse Raphael and a show about Predictions for the Millennium. It wasn't an accident that I saw these shows. I was ill that day. It was yet another synchronistic event that would add a piece to the puzzle of my mysterious life.

The day of the service, the church was filled to the brim with worshipers; from lay people to nuns and priests. An air of expectancy filled the church. I was surprised to find video cameras there as well. On the front altar was the now famous portrait. I confidently strode to the side altar of the Blessed Mother and, for some reason, prayed, or rather, demanded a miracle. I figured, if the Blessed Mother gave them a miracle, I wanted one as well! I then took my seat in front of the church facing Her statue, waiting expectantly, but, intermittently for a sign; forgetting about my request as I watched the crowds and waited.

Though the actual ceremony hadn't started, I saw maimed and crippled people filing into a room on the side of the main altar. It was later that I found out that Estelle Ruiz, the wife, was conducting a prayer vigil for their needs. In the interim, we prayed the rosary and sang for three hours, the most I had spent in church since my painful divorce of a twenty-six year marriage! I was getting restless, and it was terribly warm on that hot summer day. Finally, Mrs. Ruiz came onto the podium. She was a woman in her mid-fifties, modestly dressed in a neat white blouse and slacks. She looked like your idealized version of a kindly middle-aged grandmother with curly short gray hair. Her face was serene with an ever present smile.

She spoke of eventful happenings in their life, based on faith that changed their family, who had modern-day problems we all face with children. Their family was now at peace. I listened intently and took it down in shorthand. The message was that the Blessed Mother was coming to New York to lift the veil of darkness that covered the goodness of well-intentioned people. She also said to encourage children to pray, for their prayers would go directly to Heaven without any intercession. And not to pray for candy or other frivolous things but to pray for priests and peace, for we were in serious times.

Before I went to church that day, I received a notice from my lawyer that my divorce agreement was finalized. I took note of that as I joined the line of worshipers after the services in greeting Mrs. Ruiz. I recall my exact words... "May I hug you, for you're the closest person to Mary on this Earth?" She stretched out her arms and embraced me in a tender, comforting hug. I shared with her my pain and grief about my divorce; a divorce that came after many years of soul searching, confusion and finally the tough decision to end the marriage. It caused me a great deal of angst; especially for separating our children, and that I was the first ever to divorce in my family. Add to that the first female, Catholic one at that, and the total produced tremendous GUILT.

The synchronicity of both the day and its' events did not escape me. I was in a great deal of pain that day. In our wedding ceremony I had prepared a special bouquet of flowers for the Virgin, praying for a happy marriage. And now it was over. I knew I'd made the right decision not only for myself, but also for my ex-husband and our three children. But divorce is hard and leaves permanent scars on families. Ours was no different. Those memories and scars often caused rifts between one, or another of my three beloved children, Lisa, Andrew and Tracy. I hope and pray that this book will help somewhat in that regard, and that our family will be healed like the Ruiz's family.

My reverie ended before I could revisit the Miracle. A horn honked out in front of the motel. I was now in the present, on my way to the Dream Seminar and about to find out the connection between the miracle and meeting Leonilla. My "pregnant" dream was about to give birth in the form of a stranger from India.

CHAPTER FIVE: "CAPE COD AND BEYOND"

The shrill signal to board the bus to the Dream Seminar temporarily interrupted my reverie. However, the memory of my "miracle" remained. How can one forget such an event? The question on my mind changed from "What Is Love?" to "What does it mean?" I was on a different quest, to write a book but about what? The answer was presented to me with my deceased mother's reappearance.

"How" the medal attached to the pen was as memorable as the "Why." The Sedona couple's testimony of faith, love, healing and prayer was transcribed by myself in shorthand; a skill that remained from my former days as a secretary. After the service, a woman asked for my address and to borrow a pen. She was interested in the message from Mary that I'd transcribed. As I reached into my purse for a pen, the Miraculous Medal was attached to the pen! It wasn't attached by ordinary ways. It wasn't caught by a clip, or some sticky substance, or by a magnet - it was just there - dangling merrily as if it was pleased with itself.

I was stunned, as I waved it in amazement. I cried out to those around me, "Look, the medal is attached to the pen! What does it mean?" Someone said "You're supposed to write!" As I handed the pen to the nurse, the medal fell. It would take the next seven years of my spiritual journey and development for the book to be birthed.

For days and months on end, I questioned the meaning of the miracle. Write? Write about what? I recall attending a workshop the next day. When I told my story, the presenter, a non-Christian, crossed herself spontaneously and said I had a great deal of power. She asked me what I wanted to do with it? I was stunned! Power? Do something with it? Was this woman nuts? I brushed her words aside as if I wanted to rid myself of the thought, so fearful to me. It was OK to yearn for something, another to obtain it; for in so doing I had to OWN my POWER!

And so I searched for answers. But answers didn't come, as they hadn't when another miracle happened years before, when a bloodstain appeared suddenly on my white blouse as my aunt was sewing a button on. "Oh, Elaine, look I have pierced you!" "That's OK, Aunt Carrie." With those words, a fifty-cent sized bloodstain disappeared from my white blouse. I was astounded, as was my Aunt. Again I questioned the meaning. That questioning led me to Love, in more ways than one. It was suggested by a friend's mother of my youngest daughter, a Jehovah Witness, to read Corinthians 13 and to ask for protection. I knew from her reaction that she was fearful. I wasn't concerned about protection, I was looking for answers. Answers which I found, only I didn't know it at the time. A very simple but profound answer; that of Love. I was in too much pain from the marriage to know that I was being loved and cared for at that difficult time in my life.

My reverie continued on the bus ride to the workshop. I couldn't shake thinking about the dream and vision of Mary earlier that morning. It certainly was apt timing, more than I could ever imagine. The bus stopped at the movie theater on that hot Monday morning. As we entered the theater, the lights went out! "Hmm," I thought, "interesting opening for a Dream Seminar." Always wanting to be near the "action," I walked up to the front. From the corner of my eye I saw Leonilla sitting on the opposite side of the aisle a few rows up from where I was. "That's it! I'm going to introduce myself to her during the intermission."

I settled into my seat with my thoughts and looked around the theater and was disappointed because I didn't want to be sitting in a dark, lifeless movie theater. I wanted to be where we usually went - the wonderful open space of the high school near the National Seashore. I'd drive to the school, after the morning workshop, grab my beach gear and walk the mile or so to the beach. It was another one of my yearly "mountain" rituals.

During the intermission, I saw Leonilla. There she was, sitting alone in the lobby, looking quite self-contained with a smile on her face. It was almost as if she were reading my resistant thoughts. My curiosity couldn't be contained any longer. I approached her rather sheepishly and introduced myself. "Hello, I'm Elaine. Are you the young lady all the way here from India?" She smiled knowingly and invited me to sit down with her. I'll never forget my first question to her. "What work do we have to do with one another?" "Time will tell" was her wise and knowing answer. With that, we began a fast-paced conversation like long-lost friends, till intermission ended.

19

An appointment was made to meet that very afternoon after she rested and meditated. Already, I was receiving some lessons. Rest? Meditation? They were foreign entities to me at that time. Once back at the motel, I was raring to go; wanting to find out who this young woman was, and what did we have to learn from each other. I could hardly rest, and anyway, I hated staying in cramped, closed quarters on such a beautiful sunny day. Space has always been important to me, in more ways than one, since my days of sleeping on a "branda", (Italian for 'daybed') in the living room till I was sixteen. I yearn for space, instead I receive constriction.

I strolled the pebbly path to the pool and tried to remain calm, as I was excited to again meet with this fascinating young woman. My mind wandered to the morning's talk; thinking again about my dream. But not for long, as Leonilla appeared across the lawn to the pool where I sat. In fact, she was skipping! She exuded joy! Much to my surprise she said she had completed a visualization in which she forgave her parents. I was almost twice her age and still hadn't begun to even think about forgiving my parents. The pain was great, the burden heavy, but evidently not heavy enough to let go of through forgiveness. I didn't realize that at the time. I knew nothing about the tools of forgiveness, such as bodywork, visualization or even that I had the power to do so! I had used my power to heal people. Did I have any left for myself?

We'd meet daily after the seminar. Conversations flowed especially about spirituality. She telling me her story and I mine. One day, we hopped into my car and headed up to Provincetown. We had decided to go on a Whale Watch, which was something I had never done. Though I had been up to the Cape for five years now, try as I might, I couldn't get the courage to go. When she heard my fears of being on a boat, Leonilla said that "it was about time you faced that fear." And so it was, simple as that.

Having some time before sailing, we toured the numerous shops. In one store, Leonilla quietly asked to look at some tiny gold earrings. I heard the lady quote the price and saw the look on her face. In the meantime, I was trying on some earrings and had taken off the gold ones I had given my mother, who hadn't accepted them. I was hurt, but later realized that it was a symptom of her being unable to take in any loving gesture. I seldom took them off, as a remembrance of her.

Something, but more like, someone, spurred me to offer them to Leonilla, which wasn't like me. "Leo, (by now my fond nickname for her) I think my earrings would look well on you. I'd like you to have them." Once offered, I knew why the act of giving is as much a gift for the giver as the receiver. Another of love's lessons which started with the dream of Mary. Mother, mothers, mothering. And love! I had come to the Cape for "mare," "mother", and mothering. I received both.

Once on the boat, we eagerly scanned the horizon for whales. It was great fun to see the people on board rush from one side of the deck to the other, for a whale sighting. Most of the time, it was futile. At one point, we remained by ourselves. Suddenly, a huge whale was by our side spraying us. I shouted to Leo, "Either the whale is peeing on us or blessing us!" With Leo at my side, I'm sure it was the latter.

At the end of the day, we headed to shore. We sat in the back of the boat. The combination of swiftly churning waters created a beautiful visual pattern, as well as a peaceful sense of serenity and rhythm in my body. That, and the setting sun, presented a very special moment and image in time for me. I looked over at Leo. She was deep in mindfulness. Our eyes met. We both silently gave reverence to the moment. Words weren't necessary. We both just knew it was a special time with our Creator. I'll never forget that wonderful memory. I noticed that Leo seemed to be "in this world but not of this world." She appeared to be in constant communication with God. This was one of them. There was none of the usual busy chatter people make. It wasn't necessary.

We'd walk the beach early in the morning; Leo quiet, I uncomfortable with the silence. Hard as it was, I respected it. In turn, the seashore's magnificent panorama quieted my busy mind. I found a sense of harmony in walking silently along the sandy beach, feeling energized by the fresh air. At times the silence would be interrupted by Leo bounding, leaping, and skipping joyfully. I smiled a knowing smile, learning again from her spontaneity and appreciation of life. Her free spirit was contagious.

Leo worked with the untouchables in the southern part of India. She also was a trainers' trainer. She developed a curriculum to enhance women's self-esteem, and worked on demystifying negative myths that disempowered women. She humbly spoke about receiving a medal of honor from the French Ambassador. He compared her to Teilhard DeChardin, the noted philosopher, priest, and anthropologist. She also spoke of her meetings with Mother Teresa.

Our time together was filled with joy. So much so that it brought up my negativity. Her demeanor remained steady; mine wavered as the ego did battle with the heart. I had to work through my resentments, inadequacies and generosity issues. I began to see that though she was highly esteemed in her country, she needed nurturing, and mothering. "No wonder the Blessed Mother came to me. Now I understand! I needed to comfort a stranger visiting a foreign land. Leo had indicated that the priests at the monastery where she resided were apprehensive of her visit to America. She persevered, insisting the trip was necessary. Besides, she'd needed a break from her hard work. With a sense of pride, I realized the gift I had received in being connected to her.

Time flew by and the week was soon over. I'd had such a wonderful, though unexpected, time; a time that was now ending. Endings were hard for me, and I voiced that to Leo. She replied with wisdom beyond her years: "We've been to the mountain. We've seen God. Now we have to climb down to earth and do His work." Those words still resonate with me. "That's what being in the flow means," I thought. I learned a great deal about letting go that week. Other lessons of Love and Joy were learned as well. Most importantly, was when she said to me "Elaine, you are both loved and loving." I treasure those words from such a spiritual being, who knew at five years old that she wanted to do God's work, a work that continues to this day.

When we parted, I had a sense she didn't like to write. Sure enough, after the first short letter, in response to my voluminous "babbling," four or five years went without answers to my letters. My fear, my projection, was that she had been killed, for Leo truly was an activist. I was wrong. After questioning persons who traveled to that part of India to see an Avatar named Sai Baba, I received my answer. I was told that if you connect with this holy being, you would receive an answer in a dream. I wrote to Sai Baba. Soon after, I saw Leo's face in a dream, her eyes uplifted as if looking to God. I interpreted it incorrectly thinking that she had died. Years passed, and again I asked Sai Baba. A week later Leo wrote to me saying for some strange reason, she wanted to be connected to me. She wrote that "by now I'm sure you have found out what your life's purpose is." And then she asked not if, but "when am I coming to India." Soon.

The lessons I'd learned with Leo about letting go became apparent to me as I returned to work. It felt like culture shock. Time at the Cape further strengthened my conviction to leave. Now I was sure that my soul and spirit were being killed off. Five months later, I left there for a part-time, temporary job that was the turning point of my professional career. Again, it happened synchronistically.

I had been speaking to my friend, Elide about needing to leave. As usual, she was angry at my inability to move and volunteered a lead on a job she herself was interviewing for. Elide is a weird sort of friend, she can be as generous as that, and in the turn of a phrase, be quite critical, though warranted. I was amused that Elide called the Director the two times I was being interviewed. I got the job and quickly left the Bronx, my parents, and the toxic outpatient unit. I was very happy. I had a shorter commute, and a chance to hone my skills at psychotherapy. Indeed, the day was packed with a client every forty-five minutes.

What I found interesting about taking a leap of faith was that it strengthened me for life's continuous challenges. I also discovered, much to my amusement, that once I walked in faith, people around me were faced with THEIR security fears. I remained calm. I didn't want "a job." I wanted a place of my own, without administrative hassles. I wanted an office facing the Hudson River. I wanted the opportunity to live on one side of the river, and work on the other. My dream was answered when a colleague introduced me to an office in Tarrytown. That was the beginning of another of life's mysteries. As I opened the door to the office the very first day, and looked at the river, and thought of my accomplishments, I said "There's something else." The strange remark was to bear fruit two years later when I was hit by a car while crossing the street, three months to the day that my beloved mother had died, and three weeks after I had received the mystical vision of beings "reordering" my spine, as well as hearing the sounds of that reordering like a "chunk, chunk, chunk" of machinery being lined up. My life soon took another jarring turn, one completely out of the realm of anything I'd ever have experienced.

CHAPTER SIX: "MYSTERY"

My mother's life, as well as her pain, revolved around secrets and shame, both lodged in the body. Secrets of a child born before me and before she married my father. I wondered who was the father? According to psychics, that child, a girl, is still alive. I have yet to find her. My search hasn't produced results at present because I don't know her first name which is the key to finding her. My mother had several abortions as well; one, I believe before I was born, and one after. Her body bore the secrets, and they festered into disease. I feared that happening to me, and so bodywork is very important.

Her pain gave me the gift of life. I became a Social Worker; tending to people's minds, and bodies. My brother became a medical doctor, also tending to people's bodies, and minds. There was a direct correlation between my mother's secret, and subsequent illnesses that resulted in healing in the next generation. And, in turn, I hope do the same with succeeding generations. Whether we know it consciously or unconsciously, the body knows!

My struggle is also with my body, in different ways than my mothers. Several years ago, on my birthday, I decided to take a workshop that spoke not only to the body, but soul as well. I would say to friends, "I want to find out about this thing below my neck." I feared my body would take on illness as my mother's had. The workshop on mind/body connections was another step of a deepening spiritual process. I thought about our bodies being the only "thing" we enter the world in, and the body's wisdom is what we need to heal. The body can be a prisoner or it can offer freedom. We yearn for freedom; it is the body that can give it to us for it tells us what is wrong.

Unfortunately, my mother didn't know how to rid herself of her deep, dark, silent, shameful and depressive pain. She was locked into an era that encapsulated women, embodying them in their homes, but not their bodies - with mind, body and soul prisoners without light. Raising children, and tending to family was "allowed", having a voice was not. And the body contained their suffering.

Today, something in my body was hurting and related to having a voice. It started last week with a phone call from Lisa, my eldest daughter: "Hi, Mom! I'm calling from Baton Rouge. I just received

24

First Place and Honorable Mention for two of my feature stories."
Now three generations were united in victorious triumph. Lisa, my
eldest, continues the writing passion hidden in me for so long. Lisa,
my eldest, who asked me when she was ready to board the train to go
to college - "Mom, what do I do well?" Little did I know that the
quick reply I gave her would be the biggest gift, besides her birth.
Lisa went to Journalism School, and many years later began her
journey to her self, in becoming a reporter.

Elide was visiting me at the time. We had been sitting at the
dining room table in my beloved "love nest" apartment that I came to
ten years ago after my divorce. We were having dinner when Lisa
called. She and I both spoke with Lisa, caught up in her excitement,
now united with our own. I sent her flowers that day indicating how
very proud I was of her. She never acknowledged them. Where does
this pain go? The same place it went with my mother - in the cellular
level of the body where it festers as it did with my Mom.

I know it's all in love's service, but terribly painful. The
juxtaposition of excitement and pain struck me. Exciting moments
are what I call "The fires of desire;" that of life's ever-burning flames;
flames that trigger off in us the memory and recognizance of who we
really are. Then the fire burns even higher, prodding and nudging us
on - to God. "Did my mother experience any of this in her lifetime?"
I wonder aloud. I have no answers. And what do I do with the pain?
I turn it into negative excitement, foolishly thinking that would end
the hurt. But I'm only deceiving myself, for it then goes into eating
addictions with deepening pain.

On the positive side, the same excitement exists in my body
whenever I think of my lover, strangely similar to yearnings to attend
college. It's really the same quest. The quest to know oneself. I
graduated high school at sixteen, unsure of myself as to what I wanted
to be or do. Instead of continuing on to college, I became a secretary,
but the yearning to learn continued. I went to college at forty-seven,
the same year Lisa entered her first year as a Journalism major. One
day I sat in the library and gazed out the window. "It" suddenly hit
home. "IT" was finally happening! The dream, the yearning to attend
college produced fruit, after thirty-one years.

Unbeknownst to my conscious mind, fear was revisiting me,
asking me to walk in faith. I had won a legal battle that I had been

putting off for a long time. I didn't want to deal with it. Not dealing with it only further burdened me. I finally addressed it, went to court, and was elated afterwards. The day was gorgeous. I decided to stroll in the fashionable shops nearby. While browsing, the word "sigmoidoscopy" came to me. I was puzzled and furious; puzzled because I couldn't imagine the trigger for this word, and furious because I had been in a wonderful upbeat mood. A call to my brother, an internist, further upset me. Not only did I need to take the exam, but family medical history indicated a colonoscopy was necessary!

I questioned the meaning of this in my life, at this time. Oftentimes, I recalled Jim, my shaman friend, saying just stay with the experience and the answers will come. Friends suggested I meditate and ask my body. I did. "Cleaning out, letting go" came to me. I called Jim, and made an appointment to do energy work. The night before the test, Jim and I worked over the phone. I receiving, he sending, incredible and powerful healing energy.

"Elaine, there's nothing there," as he looked into my energy field. I never understood how he did it but know that he did. I trusted Jim from the first moment I met him. So like Jim, always so loving and reassuring. In fact, he indicated that his "guides" had told him that the procedure would be taken out of the surgeon's hands. Needless to say, one couldn't say that to a doctor. I just let it go and rested in faith. I was glowing the next day with wonderful energy. Everything went well. I've come to understand that the blocked energy of emotions over the lawsuit had now been freed up. Therefore, psyche was urging me to "revisit" and let go of even further old, decaying memories. I was being prepared for new birth, new growth.

Immediately after the test, and prior to it, I had so much energy that I drove myself to and from the doctor's office. According to my friends, that was unheard of. To illustrate the wisdom of the body and importance of readiness for new growth; immediately after the test, a realtor and prospective tenant rang the bell. I had just gotten back from the test. A half hour later I was looking for a new place to live, something I had been wishing for a long while. The Universe had given me a message, and most importantly, I WAS ABLE TO HEED IT!

The recent pain related to Lisa's call, coupled with the elation of the medical test results, had a ripple effect, for I yearned to see my lover, and called him. It had been six months since last we met. Time seems to have another meaning for both of us. There isn't any pressure other than to call when one feels the time is right. The time was now. "Hi, I just cleaned up my shit. I had a colonoscopy." He answered the phone with his pleasant voice. I loved his voice. It did something to my loins. I pictured a smile spreading over his wonderful lips. I adore that man. We both laughed at my statement. He honed in on my excitement. I was elated. We quickly made time to see one another as soon as possible.

The call also was prompted by relief. My body felt free. I had cleared out major energy pathways from old traumas that reside in cellular memory, especially with dark memories of the past ignited by Lisa's phone call and subsequent pain. I was ready for the next step. My body had given me the signal to let go. It was gently urging me on to my Higher Self.

Before seeing my lover and energized from recent events, I decided to take care of other rather unpleasant business. "Ugh, Income Tax Day!" Fears about money issues now in my face. I hadn't been working since the accident and was upset about it. "Forms are long since mailed out." "Get that stuff out of the way so I can go to nature." I was talking to myself, now both nervous and excited at the same time about life in general. I went to nature to put things in order; order of mind so I can write, think and integrate events. I went to a quiet spot at a lake. Trees are beginning their natural cyclical rhythm of opening their buds anew to the call of spring. A group of developmentally disabled children are in a bus to view this beautiful natural site. The driver, oblivious of the respect natures' quiet ways demand, is blaring the radio. I told myself "People like him don't stay long." "There's nothing here for them," or so I think. Nothing but peace and quiet, sun and air and sweet natural smells and sounds of nature.

"Hmmm, not a a peep out of the birds! Where are the birds," I thought. My mind was deep in thought about recent events. The next chapter of my book was on my mind. The title now formulated. I had meditated, and asked for a sign if it was the correct title. A few minutes later, I received an answer. The phone rang. There was no

27

one there.   Only my mother calling me from a REALLY LONG DISTANCE! I smiled with a sense of knowing. "Hi, Mom, I'm glad you like the title." And so, I begin anew and refreshed, with recently found order in my life; order and a newly found purpose.   I felt energized and the voltage was invigorating.

A crow sits on a log, then crosses the road foraging for food. There's another, and another there. In silence. Silence sometimes speaks louder than words. Silence is freedom. I think my mother also yearned to be free, but didn't know how to obtain freedom. She also yearned to share her secret. Yet no one would, or could hear her. Our ears had heard enough pain. I choke back the tears as I hear the bird calls, awakening to the glory of the day, as I now imagine my mother awakening to her glory, to her essence. "Too late for this lifetime, Mom," the tears now slowly streaming down my face.   A young pony-tailed boy stops his car to take pictures alongside the lake's fire house. It's a pretty scene. A hawk is circling overhead. I marvel at his wingspan and ability to soar high and free. I wished my mother could have done the same.

CHAPTER SEVEN: "FAMILY"

My mother seemed to have had happy times, and came from a very close-knit family. Mom was the eldest female in the Picchioni family, which was well rooted in Italian culture and heritage. Women at home, men at work. Her parents, Severino and Alma, had five children: Paul, Marguerite, Florence, William and Peter. Severino was Italian born and raised. Her father was also one of five brothers, and a sister. Alma was a French orphan, raised in Italy. Her family history remains a mystery.

Severino was a foreman in construction; the same work that would kill him. A crane fell on him, injuring his left arm as he was directing his workers. His arm had to be amputated and he died the next day from blood poisoning. My mother was in school when it happened. She was twelve years old. My grandmother had died two years earlier from a fall in their backyard while hanging out clothes. Mother and unborn child landed on a pointed stake. The unborn child was full term. My mother was ten. Both times going to school, and both times coming home to find one, then the other parent irretrievably gone. I can only imagine with horror the searing pain; enough pain to lose hope, over and over again. At first early on in life, and then continuing almost relentlessly to her death.

Two years ago, when she came home from her last hospital stay, she recalled memories of childhood. How her father would take them out to the park. How her mother would bake homemade apple pies. How sweet life must have been. How swift it changed. Orphaned within two years. How sad I couldn't be more objective of her when she was alive, or compassionate. How fortunate to still have some memories and relatives to piece her story together. How sad I couldn't hear her few words; ones of any substance or emotion. For words filled with emotion were used sparingly by her; its' silent voiceless meaning contained in her body.

The children were now orphaned and abandoned; voiceless and traumatized. The trauma played out in their separate life dramas. They were a close bunch but without a mother, who did they have to cling to, to tell their joys or fears to? Aunt Jennie, my grandfather's sister came to care for them. She was tough and burly, but as I recall, loving. She must have cared for them, but could never replace their mother.

Soon after, my grandfather wed his brother's sister-in-law. Grandma Rose, a thin, frail, quiet woman, had never married. She treated the children royally. My mother, as with all the siblings, adored her. She was shy, easy-going and the adoration was mutual. She spoiled them, if one can "spoil"five traumatized, vulnerable, fearful and no longer innocent children. However, some semblance of peace reentered the family home; but only for two years. And once again, the children's world was devastated with their father's death.

Grandma Rose died at a ripe old age in a nursing home in Staten Island. She chose not to live with any of the children she had raised. Instead, she went to live in Brooklyn with her sister and brother-in-law. I recall the long trip to Brooklyn, listening in the back seat to my mother speaking with poignancy at not being able to care for her. My mother loved her so. I share a similar pain since my mother's death, the pain of not being able to care for a parent as that parent cared for you.

Once at the immaculate two family house in Brooklyn, I recall running up the long outdoor flight of stairs to kiss Grandma Rose, Aunt Mary and Uncle Mike. We'd be cuddled, hugged, squeezed and adored, as well as showered with money and candy. We'd huddle into Grandma's small room where she'd pour her heart out to her daughter. My little ears would hear the pain as well. After the talk, grandmother, daughter and myself would file into the large kitchen where Uncle Mike would hold court. Once finished, we'd all pile into the livingroom where carpet upon carpet, and plastic upon plastic would impale the furniture.

As we'd leave, there would be sad "Goodbyes," money in my brother's and my hands, and cookies and candy in our bellies. We knew we were loved by her. I adored Grandma. She was very gentle, and truly special person.   I cherish the memory I have of her, encapsulated in the delicate rose china plate that resides over the sink, comforting me. I miss her quiet, ever accepting presence.

The ride home along Ocean Parkway was comforting, as my younger brother, Gerald, and I sat in silence in the back seat. Mother would drive, father in the passenger seat and the same conversation on the way there would be repeated, this time with the inclusion of how cheap Uncle Mike was and how he really didn't love Grandma Rose. Our tender ears didn't miss a word. To this day, my brother and I never speak of those visits.

Gone now are the trips to Brooklyn, as well as the Staten Island Ferry ride to see Grandma Rose in a nursing home. I used to love the Ferry. I especially recall the time we went on Palm Sunday when I took my three children. There was a late snow on the ground, with the small buds of yellow daffodils, poking their noses through the newly fallen snow. Those were good days. They were innocent days, now long lost.

My mother was very close to her mother. She had Grandma Rose's rocking chair till a year before she died. She'd sit by the livingroom window, rocking back and forth as her crippled, arthritic hands created magnificent knitted treasures for me, my children, and any baby that entered the family. How she must have relived her earlier years with each stitch. There were doll's dresses, hats, sweaters, booties and the famous Afghans - so many of love's creations that spewed forth until the time came when she no longer had that outlet. The hands she so freely gave of were no longer viable. At that point, she'd spend her time, and her mind, occupied by TV and crossword puzzles. Her mind was forever sharp.

My memory is of her sitting in the new rocker my father had bought for her eighty- fifth birthday. She had used Grandma Rose's for a very long time, until my father no longer could repair it, or my mother could no longer stand the random ties and cords holding it together. Then the order would go out "Jerry, throw it away." And Jerry did her bidding.

The lineage continues with my youngest daughter, Tracy, requesting Grandma's chair. But it's hard to ask my father for his wife's rocker with her shopping bag still hanging over one arm. I've asked several times, and several times he'd have an excuse not to give it to me. I promised the rocker to Tracy. Someday she'll have it, along with her memories.

My mother had been hospitalized for several months. I decided to give her a celebration for her birthday. My father proudly presented her with the new rocker. I recall her sitting in it, dressed in the beige new dress with white lace collar I bought her. She liked beige, as well as grey. Grey was the color she wore for her wedding. She purposely chose that color. Grey was the color her mother wore when she was buried. I believe a large part of my mother died that day as well. And again, and again, many times over, with "baby pains," hers and other voiceless children.

My children, my two cousins, Marilyn and Terry, and their daughters, Deanna, Dawn and Samantha came from New Jersey. Hardly anyone in our family crossed the imposing and almost impossible bridge, called the George Washington Bridge. When family came "on this side of the river," that remarkable feat was similar to Washington crossing the Delaware! What is that all about? Everyone knew, but didn't give it a voice, or a word - agoraphobia. The family trauma continued into the next generation in a different form, however, still crippling, still silent.

My mother looked frail, shy and visibly aged from the long and traumatic hospital stay. Her smile showed her pleasure. She wore no bra, and insisted the bulge near her midriff was her tummy; until she had to admit otherwise from our laughter. We were able to laugh, really laugh, that day. Laughter seldom was permitted in the house, silence was the silent rule, voiceless was the voice's prison. But that day was different for her entire and extended family were all there. She was always happy when family was around, for family was very important to her. As I write this my heart is tweaking with pain, the pain we all bravely, and silently, bore. The pain that burdened and depressed. The pain that kills. I recall my mother's exact words that day. "I have never felt so loved before in my life. I want to live." And live she did for two more years.

The rocking chair movement was dictated by her animated emotions. I hadn't seen her that happy in decades. It moved swiftly back and forth, gliding easily in the smooth new grooves. She began to tell us stories of yesteryear. There was no hint of the pain she bravely, and silently bore. Her eyes glistened, her mouth and smile told me she was in another dimension. Her whole body came alive. A few precious memories were welcome reprieve, both for her and her family.

I'll never forget that day and shall be telling it in my rocking chair to my children, ages and ages hence. "Two roads diverged in a yellow wood, and sorry I could not travel both...I shall be telling this with a sigh…two roads diverged in a wood, and I - I took the one less traveled by, and that has made all the difference." (Robert Frost)

CHAPTER EIGHT:
"COMING HOME - THE VISION"

After meeting Leonilla, and returning from Cape Cod, I had now left my parents along with my job. However, our connection remained as deep as ever. I'd desperately tried to lead my own life, be a dutiful daughter, doting parent and follow my dreams, whatever they may be. All this caused me a great deal of anxiety. My private practice was slowly growing. I continued energy healing work with Madeline, as well as funding further energy experiences with Jim, my newly found male mentor/shaman and "soul coach." Concurrently, the deepening spiritual path, with numerous mystical experiences led me to a retreat.

I had met Jim at Kripalu, a Yoga center in the majestic Berkshires in Massachusetts. He was, I believe, sent to me for a deepening of my spiritual consciousness. Initially, my resistance kicked in, for I instantly knew there was serious and profound work to be done by the both of us. Because of that, I avoided him for the first couple of days, as with Leo, but I soon knew that our work needed to commence. Commence it did, and continued through daily long distance phone calls, for several years, which were immensely healing, and took me to another dimension of shamanic realms.

The year was 1996. February was upon us with Valentine's Day again fast approaching and no permanent committed relationship in my life. I was, however, looking forward to my first retreat at Mt. Saint Alphonsus, in Esopus, NY. The brochure appealed to me, and I thought it would break up winter's monotony. The topic was "Thinking With the Heart/Feeling With the Mind." I had spoken to Jim about it. He replied "Hmmm, should be an interesting experience." "Think so?" I said, hopefully. I had been feeling quite lethargic and needed an energy boost. My legs could hardly carry me. What I didn't know then was that I was carrying my mother's last passion.

I arrived early and was astounded at the enormity of it's castle-like exterior. It was situated on magnificent grounds with rolling hills, ponds and streams overlooking the majestic Hudson River in upstate New York. The castle formerly housed a monastery. Its' architecture recalled earlier days of Byzantine splendor. The solidity of its' granite structure matched the religious traditions of Christianity.

I entered the building and climbed the imposing marble staircase. I saw a long hallway framed with row upon row of pictures of saintly images. Each footstep seemed to emblazon echoes on the exquisite marble floor, seemingly awakening memories of devout priests in silent prayer. Regal, tall, stained-glass windows shown with the beauty of the afternoon sunlight. I saw or heard no one. Quiet reigned supreme and I welcomed the respite from the world's din and clamor. I walked down the hallway, door after door closed to the intrusive eyes of strangers. There was a deep sense of reverence and contained, but stimulated energy in me, that this sacred place had awakened. My footsteps became more solemn and respectful, each one seemed to deepen and restore my long lost faith that I had abandoned with my divorce. After a while, I was met by a pretty young, trim woman. She was dressed in jeans, her hair in a single, long braid. I introduced myself and found her name to be the very same one of the character in a book I had started, along with my new job, on the psychiatric unit in the Bronx, near my childhood home. The book was unfinished. There were two main characters, "Elaine" and "Elisa". "Elaine," of course, represented myself, as the young, Italian female, quite religious, with the "rosary beads and white gloves," I used to say, to describe what felt like a former lifetime. The "Elaine" that would grow into a perceptive and pursuing young woman who worked in the Mental Health Field, one who had great success with clients, whether they be schizophrenic, bipolar or "other." Sickness of the soul wasn't foreign to me, or my client. "Elisa" represented the grown, mature, wise, integrated woman I aspired to become.

I was puzzled as to why the book was unfinished. I had gone through my childhood, daughter of Margaret and Gerolamo Cordani, older sister to my brother, Gerald, my stint in mental health and substance abuse, my wonderful lover, and tumultuous experience at my youngest daughter's wedding. An attempt was made to write about the failed twenty-six year marriage, but that never materialized. The pain was still too great to address.

Now, at sixty years old, I've integrated both characters! Integration was the piece and attained by these past few years of really feeling traumas during healing energy work. The process cannot be rushed. When the time is right, and only then, and in God's time, not ours.

My thoughts soon evaporated from this fleeting uprooted memory. Elisa, the "real" Elisa was speaking to me. I had been daydreaming. "Did you see the chapel," she said. replied "No," wondering why that would be important. Elisa pointed across the hallway to huge, ornate, magnificent doors of said chapel. I hadn't noticed them before. I had no idea what was to come next.

I swung open the door and was greeted by two magnificent 16th Century life-sized marble angels! Each angel was embracing a font containing holy water. I was stunned by their very real presence. I spontaneously hugged them as I would a dear, long lost friend. In shock, I was drawn to the compelling domed ceiling with its' imposing stained glass. I saw the Pelican, a symbol of Divine Love, and the Holy Spirit. I had never seen a church more beautiful than this chapel. The magnificent exterior was equally matched by its' interior. I saw a woman on the side altar meditating at the statue of the Sacred Heart of Jesus. She was ON the altar. What boldness, what wonderful integration of Eastern and Western traditions! What a true blending of spirituality. Samantha was to become a welcomed friend that weekend. I wept for joy. I felt as if I had come home - home TO heart and home TO my soul! I instantly knew that the tears weren't shed just for its beauty alone. There was a proclamation here, with much more to come. I left Elisa, speechless and spent several hours there in prayer of gratitude for my homecoming; so long yearned for, so surprisingly announced! I had now come to both celebrate and embrace Elaine and Elisa, at that moment.

Another life-changing event happened during a profound mystical experience the next day in a group meditation. The night before coming to the Mount, I found myself taking off my treasured onyx heart pin and set it on my altar. I thought it odd, noted it, and let it go. That night a vision of Jesus appeared. That was really odd! I had many occurrences with the Blessed Mother, but none with Jesus. I sensed that Jesus was representative of a more balanced male/female psyche, that of anima and animus in Jungian thought.

The group met in the tower of this huge edifice. As I climbed up the steps to the tower, my mind went to Jung's tower in which he spent his later years in meditation and reflection. This tower had windows on each of the four sides and the view was breathtaking. It overlooked the Hudson River. The mood in the large room was enhanced by the congenial atmosphere of like-minded people; smells of incense and candles lingered in one's nostrils and very being. I entered into the group meditation, which was conducted by Elisa.

She started by asking us to close our eyes and breathe deeply... "You're in a boat, lost on the ocean. You find yourself on an island. There's a tree. Around the tree are fourteen stones." She stopped, leaving us to our own imagination. As soon as I closed my eyes, I saw a scene. It was as if I had turned on a TV set and was looking at colored images. It happened that fast. I saw a tree. It was bare. I then saw one bird. It had a red silk ribbon in its beak. The bird tied it around a newly budding tree. More birds and garlands emerged, until soon the tree was in full festive bloom.

The vision continued. I was in awe at the rapidity of the expansion. It was as if something, or someone, had taken over the process. I just sat back and watched my "tv show." There was a circus tent complete with monkeys as well as other animals. I was circling above this splendor dressed as a fairy with a magic wand. I was flying all over sending love, light and joy. A city appeared. And more trees. The scenario ever expanding. A skyscraper appeared. It was then that I took over. I didn't want a skyscraper in MY vision! A river in Africa appeared. People were paddling their canoes. Joy was rampant till suddenly there appeared a scene reminiscent of the movie "Waterworld." War broke out. The Atomic Bomb exploded but it didn't spread for Heaven intervened with a mighty shield which suffused the toxins.

I began to sob as I saw an outline of a large red heart, with a dot in the middle. I stared at the dot. It grew larger. I was experiencing mystical rapture. My breathing was shallow, my heart pounding. I was fully conscious on one level, as well as experiencing a very different plane of consciousness on another. The tiny dot in the center began to expand larger and larger, its' red color increasing in intensity. The heart again blossomed, like a tree, only this time with exquisite long stemmed red roses. I cried out words of awe. I felt my entire being, especially my heart, expanded, and then lifted up to the

Heavens. My body felt as if it were being raised from the seated chair. It was the most incredible experience I had ever had.

At that point, I saw a very powerful symbol, one with great meaning to myself. It was the letter "Y." I again sobbed for only a few hours ago while coming up the road from the river, I had seen a woman and child walking. The woman held a beautiful piece of driftwood in the shape of a "Y." I wanted that driftwood, for seeing it then, as well as now, recalled the memory established in a bodywork session that produced this powerful image, so deeply imbedded in my psyche. In that image, I was the lower portion, the stem, with mother and father each part of its upper portions; mother in pink, father in blue and I in white. It reminded me that I am never alone. That my parents, and Jesus and Mary, were always with me. With that I saw Jesus' face and the Crown of Thorns. His face was similar to the Shroud of Turin's image. I then saw Mary. However, she appeared in the form of Elisa. No matter how strange this may sound, I have come to believe that Mary actually was in Elisa's form when Elisa directed me to the Chapel. My heart continued pounding, breathing shallow and rapidly. Jesus and Mary were holding my hands. I was given a glimpse of Heaven with a beautiful blue sky, doves flying everywhere, and the glorious Rising Sun. A gold, circular band appeared above the clouds. I felt tremendous joy and much playfulness as I heard the words "Knock and it shall be answered. Seek and you shall find. Ask and it shall be given to you."

I had certainly received a loving Valentine's Day present. Afterwards, people in the group came to me to find out about my meditative experience, for I was aware they had to have heard me gasping in ecstasy. But I was too exhausted to speak at that point. I wanted to return to the chapel, for in that meditation, I truly experienced, for the first time the "realness" of Jesus and Mary. They were no longer seen as beings I sometimes prayed to. I now KNEW their very real presence in my life. I was to carry that vision as I had carried my mother's passion. It was to prepare me for what was to come, for my mother died two months' later. I was away at the time when she fell. In some strange fashion, I was prepared for her death as if my body knew before I did. In another way, I wasn't. For all the many days and years that I felt I had been there for her, death came as "a thief in the night." One is never prepared for Death's final moments. Funny how Life is. No matter how vigilant one is, Life has a way of having the ultimate controls.

CHAPTER NINE: "LINEAGE"

Now, a year later, on Valentine's Day, I attended the same retreat. I'm first again - this time in walking the labyrinth. The labyrinth is a maze, first used in the 12th Century, and recently revised as a religious meditative practice. Many European churches, including Chartres Cathedral in France, have labyrinths embedded in the floor design. The purpose was to enable worshipers unable to travel to Mecca or Jerusalem on a spiritual pilgrimage, to pattern their devotion in the form of walking this maze-like path.

I readily accepted this internal challenge. Prior to walking the path, I received the word "lineage" in the exercise preparing us for the labyrinth. I was puzzled as to what that might mean but now understood the connection. At first I walked hesitantly, feeling dizzy both from anxiety and excitement. About a quarter of the way, I glanced at the red heart that was in the center. I began to sob with a deep sense of knowing, I knew not what about. Instinctively, I raised my hands in a prayer-like stance and took off my heart pin, the same one I wore the year before. Holding it reverently in my hand, I approached the center. Once there, words, known but not yet spoken, said but unsaid, were formulated deep in my heart and soul. I soon realized it was a letting go of the past. I reached the center, with its' heart image. My pulse quickened. It was as if I, all at once, was in the past, present and future, at the same time. Another part of the mystery had been actualized. The path was now firmly set for my new life, both present and, future as well. I sensed a resolution as I reached the end. Confident and deep in process; my steps were now solid and quickening. I sought quiet, wanting to both carry and further explore this tenuous feeling. I entered the next room that had beautiful large and imposing wood-beamed ceilings. The room overlooked the hills and valleys of Upstate New York, now covered in pure, icy, sparkling snow. To my left stood a large chalkboard. Just what I needed. Deep in thought, I again confidently strode to it as my process continued.

I began to draw with my non-dominant hand knowing this would help surface unconscious thoughts. What I drew was the symbol for infinity, the figure eight. I stayed with this process of random drawing, guided solely by intuition, for a half hour. People began to congregate in the room. I continued, unfazed. The setting sun cast eerie and interesting shadows on nature's magnificence of newly fallen snow. The trees were ice covered, the snow glistening warmly from the sun's rays. I was aware of the beauty as well as the importance of my current process. I kept on mentally following my hand, letting it flow freely where it wished over the blank page not trying to "make a pretty picture," but just being guided by inner knowledge. A figure emerged to the left. It was of a face that screamed in pain. I was horrified and quickly, defenses ever to the ready, changed it to the happy face of a dog. The agony in the face remains with me, its eyes burning, searing the viewer's consciousness, its mouth open in anguish. Is that me? Is that my mother? Who was it? I didn't have time to think of answers yet, for the images kept coming. To the right was the figure of a man. And, to my delight, at the lower right-hand corner was a plump image of a bird. My bird. Vita! My joyful and wonderful finch that Elide had given me! Vita meant "Life" in Italian. Indeed!

Suddenly, the chalk board groaned and interrupted my process. I was puzzled and then smiled. "OK. The universe is sending me a message." I heeded it, stopped drawing, sensing that I needed to turn to the other side. There, to my astonishment, was a poster of hundreds of different little birds similar to the multitude of birds in last years' meditation; first one, then many! I had received a validating and prophetic image with which to carry further along my path.

Marguerite/Margaret/Margherita had also set lineage in motion. She carried it throughout her life, in her womb, filled with e-motion. This, by a woman who died a year ago. A woman who carried her secret to the grave. A woman who came back for Redemption. A mother finally revealing her secret. The secret that, I feel, caused her many sicknesses. The secret - that she had a child out of wedlock soon after her parents died; the sister I have yet to meet. And so, begins another connection, more solid than in life, to my mother. And her mother, and my children, and the unborn babies that died before me; all united in the mystery of our family's pain and sorrow, from forgiveness, to Love! United now, not as mother to daughter, but woman to woman, a daughter finally able to give back what she had received from her mother; thereby completing the cycle of life full circle. "As so above, so below."

I mentioned to my mother several years before her death that I was writing a book. Little did I know that the notion of her book took seed as well. One day she announced "I'm writing a book too!" And write she did. I never read it while she was alive. I couldn't bear to hear her pain. My mom worked as a bookkeeper at Consolidated Laundries on 96th Street in New York. A woman who kept many neat records as she sat day after day in the little house in the Bronx. A woman who spent her days by the livingroom window, in her stepmother's old rocking chair, knitting Afghans, dolls dresses for her granddaughters, as well as sweaters for myself. And, later, once her hands were crippled with arthritis, doing puzzles. She would go from kitchen to livingroom during the day, and up the long, painful flight of stairs, to her bed at night, finally to rest. And, to awake the next day, to find the same flight of stairs awaiting her, the same rocking chair, the same tv, and the same husband. Marguerite had indeed set lineage in motion, for all of her sickly eighty-six years!

My mother fell during Passion week. She died on Holy Thursday. She also died on the first day of Passover. All bases were covered! She was buried the day after Easter. And, now, she has her Resurrection.

My mother was quiet, cynical, critical, and prone to depression. No one ever mentioned the word, but we just knew. All of us. The reason never spoken, silent and voiceless, but not barren, born but still contained in her womb; her constant source of pain and suffering. There were many illnesses, many diagnostic names, but none sufficient for the sickness of the soul. Oh, how pained she must have felt for the babies. That pain dominated her secret life; the life of born and unborn children. All but my brother and I were lost, either aborted or given away for others to raise. Though she indicated her childhood was a happy one, and perhaps it was prior to these events, I'm sure her own childhood was lost as well. And, of this I am most positive, dominating how I was raised. Soon after my mother died, a message came confirming that - a message during bodywork that "I'm now free to own my own life." Needless to say, that though I knew it all along, I was furious when my knowing was validated!

It was very painful growing up to have a depressed mother. For it felt, at times, that I hadn't a mother at all. At an early age I unconsciously became parent to my parent, voice to her voice, child to the unborn children, and the one that survived in myself; MY unborn child... waiting these many years to be born...waiting sixty long and painful years...almost an entire lifetime. This is my journey, one I'm sure, that I chose before I came into this world.

My mother's doctor from a prestigious NY Hospital, wrote a letter to my brother after her death. My brother had this doctor as a professor in medical college. He summed up my mother in this fashion: "I heard about your Mother's death and I am very, very sad and sorry. I met Margaret twenty-five years ago and, as you know, went through a number of illnesses with her. She was funny, feisty, difficult, judgmental and tough. But I was attached to her, teased her and really liked her very much. I lost touch with her two years ago and really have had no recent follow up...Remember, no matter how the relationship was, no matter how sick your mother may have been, you really have to grieve for a long time when a parent dies."

What mysteries did she bring to her death that she is wanting to be freed of? Dare I broach the subject with my father of unwanted children sacrificed on the altar of abortion, or still alive; to not die, but come alive in my mother's body with diseases? Dare I speak the unspeakable to generations present, past and to come? I must. For I am asked to do so. I only pray that I may speak and write the "right words" - neither slanderous, vilifying or saintly. Just like it is and was. To tell her story. For in telling of the stories lies the rebirth from ashes.

I'm sitting writing by my favorite pond in a town I used to live in before my divorce, the same town I reared my three young children in. I see a child with her mother. She appears to be about five years old. She's across the pond, tentatively walking alone in the tall grass by the water's edge, eyeing the swimming ducks. I think of my own children at that age. I think of myself at that age. I think of my mother at that age. The mother cries out to the child "Don't run." The child freezes, her body suddenly rigid, her eyes wide open with a puzzled look in them, as if to say "Why are you stopping me? I'm having fun exploring!" Always caution for girls, yet wild abandonment for boys. I remember the same caution that held me back at times through fears not of my own making.

My children played at the same pond when they were young. They went to the same library that looks out over the pond. My children crossed the same bridge over the same brook as the five-year-old. My children are grown now. I am alone now. My children are grown now. I am alone now.

The only picture I have of my mother's femininity was in her end times, one I hastily took at my son's wedding. She had just come out of my brother's car clutching a cane in one hand. She looked pretty. I hadn't seen her look like that in a long time. A slight breeze blew at the hem of her pale green chiffon dress lending a girlish charm to her bearing. Instantly, I received an image not of an old woman, but of a very young, feminine and sprightly spirited girl! "Wow", I thought reaching for my camera, "this is going to be an important picture." I had suddenly, and finally, captured the nine-year-old girl not the eighty-six-year-old mother. She presented me with that last cherished gift; a photo of her true essence and liberated spirit - freed at last! "Why didn't I acknowledge this instinctive behavior before as I did then? Why? Because no one ever takes themselves seriously in my family. It's always suffused either by smiles, sickness, or death.

In that sudden swift scene my mother presented to me what she must have been like as a young woman. I had captured the impish, outrageous, and somewhat brazen and scandalous girl and woman. I felt somehow proud of her and then realized I had captured myself as well. The unconscious self that continued her lineage. The breeze suddenly caused the dress to flutter, as if her soul were released as well. She had loved that dress; she was buried in that dress. Will I be buried in a pale green lime green chiffon dress like my mother?

It was the same dress she excitedly showed me after buying it from a catalogue as she didn't go out much in later years. I recall the day when I visited. She was so happy to describe the dress in detail, almost as if it represented something from the past. And then having me "Go up the stairs, in the cedar closet to the right that contains my house dresses and bring the dress down." Always the precise orders of what to do as if I was the five-year-old girl instead of a fully grown woman. As usual, the retort "Don't tell your father how much I spent." My father, or Her Father?

Dresses remind me of her mother's horrible and sudden death. She wore grey at her wedding in honor of her mother. Did my mother die that day as well? Was she buried in her body as her mother's body was buried in the coffin? Did her mother, in fact, commit suicide as the only way out for her, a female in a constricted generation of the early 20th Century? We shall never know, and it really doesn't matter, does it?

I'm crossing the brook now, by the library, the same brook my own children crossed, to my favorite spot by the water's edge. I sit by the large stones and ponder the two sides of the brook, one choppy, the other smooth; and finally the freely flowing water. My mind goes to the birds and the unfolding of Life's dramas. Will my children have a special picture of me before I die? And what of the baby that died before me and my sister that is alive? Will I be united with my sister? The mystery continues. I again think of the five year old child who is now united with her mother. My heart envies her, even though my mind knows otherwise. Both win out as I realize that I too am united now with my mother, across an invisible, but much more powerful bridge, and this time it's a healthy union with healthy bodies, healed bodies, and healing hearts and souls as well.

The birds are singing life's dances. I continue to reflect on the brook, one side peaceful, with innocent and childish serenity, until it goes under the bridge to the side that's choppy...As with Life.

CHAPTER TEN: "HANDS RECLAIMED"

The throbbing pain in back of my head ceased. I lie on my bed, after the meditation, depleted of energy. I just had an ecstatic experience and though in shock, I reviewed with awe what had just occurred. This meditation was different. IT summoned Me! I hadn't a choice. The energy in the back of my neck was DEMANDING my attention. I went to my sacred space, my altar, and sat waiting for a message knowing I would receive one. I soon saw a vision of myself in an Egyptian headdress that quickly changed to a Golden Crown. "I can handle that," I thought, pleased with what I saw. Once the vision ended, the experience left me lifeless. I crawled into bed.

It didn't end there. For some unknown reason my body felt as if it wanted to surrender; though to what, I didn't yet know. I closed my eyes, arms outstretched at my side, Christ-like and said "Thy Will Be Done." With that, I saw ethereal beings surround my body and draw a white sheet to my neck. Immediately, I sensed I was being prepared for "psychic surgery." I smiled said "Cool!" and let it happen. The vision of beings disappeared, and I felt and heard my entire spinal column being restructured as if it were a synchronized machine. "Chunk, chunk, chunk," were the sounds, and feelings, of discs being mysteriously reordered. On some level, I had agreed to that experience. I was ready. However, I wondered in amazement, "With all my daily fears and anxieties, usually about nothing, this happens and I'm calm." I didn't search for a meaning. In fact, I didn't need one, but simply accepted it.

For days and weeks beforehand I never felt comfortable when I'd lie down, for my body felt as if it needed to be straightened out. This incident left me stunned and feeling as if my spine were aligned by a chiropractor. "Only this was a home visit," I thought, chuckling in excitement of yet another mystery in my life. The answer, but not the reason, was to come a few weeks later, on the third month anniversary of my mother's death. While walking in a crosswalk, I was hit by a car. I was just two inches from her left bumper. The woman looked left and right to see if it was clear to make a turn, looked straight at me as she headed right into me. She hit my left side, causing a severe sprain/strain of my spine and contusions of my shoulder and neck. The pain was so intense when I came back to work three weeks later, that I knew I had to end my private practice. I lay on the couch in the waiting room and spoke to God knowingly: "You mean you want me to give up my private practice!" I did so willingly with full trust that I'd be taken care of. Indeed that was certainly the case.

Since the accident, each part of my anatomy has suffered severe pain. This continues to the present. In fact, I feel as if my entire body is under "reconstruction." The pain required treatment and physical therapy was prescribed. Once physical therapy ended, with minimal results, the orthopedist prescribed massage therapy three times weekly. He asked if I needed a referral. I declined knowing full well one would be sent to me. That night, I went to a park overlooking the Hudson where I received my gift. As I walked to my car, a woman on crutches was walking alongside me. We started talking. She knew of a massage therapist. The next day, I had an appointment with Tashi, a Tibetan expatriate.

Destiny did the rest. The universe provided what I needed. Tashi is a healer of body and soul. She was an internist and surgeon, forced to leave her beloved homeland. She escaped on foot from China's atrocities through the Himalayas to India. Tashi was a major force and "midwife" to my re-connection with my body. My neck was in excruciating pain. It was immensely alleviated with Tashi's deft handling and magical hands. We worked together for nine months and now she was about to give birth. I was left to find someone else, unknowingly, to birth another part of me.

That person was Dana whose treatment, though different was just as effective. We worked together for two months and now our work was about to end. I'd completed an incredibly important piece of bodywork. It's our last session. My hands look at me as I them almost as if for the first time. I caress them lovingly, looking at them as a newly found loving, and living friend. Words passed, eyes meeting, my body touched by Dana's hands in an embrace of connectedness and humanness. I have given birth to my neck and hands with Dana. Neck, the creative part, and hands the doer. It is no accident that prior to this work my hands had broken out, right hand mostly, with a childhood case of eczema. My hands were trying to give me a message, filled with energy, prodding me to write. It was time.

I shed long, old, waiting, wise, wet, young tears. The tears of wisdom gained, energy retrieved, life loosening up through bodily touch. Alive, well and happy. Thank you! I bow with respect to Dana, my hands in prayer-like stance. As I leave her office, I meet upon the life of the world today, not of the world to come. I'm in a different state of mind. I have new respect for my body. I feel wiser, more joyful, filled with deeply-felt love. Life outside, and people, appear somehow different. I feel as if I have a new pair of eyes as well as heightened senses. I see people in a new light. I have much more compassion for my fellow human beings. I see their pain ever more clearly. They drag their tired bodies, and their tired minds, forgetting their hungry souls, through bee-droning days, seemingly endless and mindless days of their lives. Certainly soulless days, for the soul seeks joy, satisfaction and fulfillment.

Most people are trapped in their bodies through fear. Most don't have the key to the doorway, to freedom, a freedom that is there waiting to be released through remembering and reconnecting with soul. But the key to freedom is hard won. It is THROUGH fear. Most stay in fear, accepting known pain rather than face the unknown. "Don't they know about life's process of alchemy, the knowledge of fusing experiences of spiritual traditions of various cultures, ancient and more recent, in order to understand the "substances" that create and fuel life and death, present, past and future, spirit and soul?" That IS Life! That's what we're here for! How can one learn by traveling the same road? We already know that path. We need to learn a new one! No wonder bodies are tired, they're trying to tell us something. But do we listen?

I drive to the river. The overburdened, weary, dirty, loyal Hudson River. My river. A container of my tears, hopes, joys and sorrows. A place that knows me. A place that soothes me. A place that is sacred to me. I escape and become enveloped and contained here. The waves are churning as are my emotions. The tiny sailboats, in hurried expectancy of fun times, are bobbing with the angry but alive, river. Are they angry as well? There are seagulls going about their seemingly happy lives. By going to the river, I concretize, internalize and sacredize MY HANDS! The hands that are finally free, free to write, free to feel, free to do! I feel the pulsation of alive-ness!

I return home nurturing the newly found gifts. A robin chirps outside my window, facing the teeming and unending din and scream of the highway, and the travelers on it. I'm at peace for I've gotten a piece of myself through my body, and bodywork. Cars race by my window now. There is no river outside. Only faceless, endless people caught in the web of life, in the traffic of life. Caught in the modern soulless phenomena, road rage! Do they know they can have a better life? I don't think so. At least, not many of them.

Ending the short but epic novel "Lord Of The Flies" was upsetting and alarming. Madeline had received the channeled message to read the book in order to understand my mother's life. She had received that information after my "Communion" session with her. The novel addresses good and evil. About society and how it manifests to and fro in individual psyches and behaviors, a society that had no mother and father for models, my mother's world. There are three main characters. The honest and sensitive one "Piggy", the intellectual. He made the most sense. For that, he was savagely beaten and killed...by the "beasties" in all of us, our shadow "beasties" most refuse to see but act out on. The need to "exterminate" the truth is everywhere especially in denial, the shadow's friend.

Then there's the savage Jack, the hunter, solely concerned with hunting and food. Ralph, the Chief, was concerned with "fire on the mountain" and being rescued. Was he the rescuer or was Jack? What we have here are images of spirit and matter, played out in savagery. But alchemy, not killings, would have served both sides. It would have helped integrate the best of each character instead of destroying people's lives. But who am I to judge, for there is a Divine Plan and purpose for each of us.

Certainly, I've encountered, faced and learned about evil. Indeed, that almost seemed easier than looking, and accepting my good side. Why is it that we are the last ones we love in a lifetime? Today I can say "I'm Jack. I'm Ralph. And I'm Piggy!" All this because of integrating another disconnected, disowned and powerful part of myself. All by the simple, and loving ritual of having my hand held physically and metaphorically which fosters actualization. We need this mirror. It helps us see ourselves, our beautiful essence as others see us. My mother had none of that. Neither did her generation.

49

They were brought up in the Depression era, and survival, as in the "Lord Of The Flies." In turn, some BECAME depression...which lasted not a decade but an entire lifetime. My mother was one of them.

Other examples of projection abound in my family. As for myself, I feel that my family abandoned me and betrayed me, but it is all in love's service. My mother was abandoned, my mother betrayed me. In turn, I abandoned and betrayed myself. Have I betrayed my children, as well? And so it goes, until one own's their personal projections by loving onself. My father doesn't think I have "the noodles" to write a book. This, an example, of his own projection of how "stupid" he feels. He is far from that. Indeed, he is quite the opposite. He's a fox! Lisa and others don't acknowledge my writing a book out of fear, denial and competition. How sad. How infuriating!

My thoughts are interrupted by sounds of school children outside. I look out the window. Tears come to my eyes. Children with AIDS are being electronically lifted to their bus, to travel to school. I pray for them, and their loving caretakers. I feel sorry for them. Do I feel sorry for myself! But then comes extraordinary events like today, and I'm re-minded, and re-connected with truth, the truth that we are never alone. The projection comes forth; of feeling sorry for self and others. Nothing but a false persona. We live a lie if we live in projections. That is what happened in my mother's generation, with false personas, false projections and the ultimate lie that of denying self, and I might add, denying God as well!

I again return to the children's drama outside my window. I'm suddenly struck with my seemingly paradoxical life circumstance. Here I am, the perennial care giver, being taken care of by others. I surprisingly welcome it, for my children were scattered around the country and had their own lives to lead. I know and understand. I tried to do the same thing, but that's not how it worked out in my family. I was the care giver to my parents and, at times, it was quite an unhealthy bond. I know it wasn't easy for my children to cut the ties where I could not.

My life goes on, however, with yet another beginning once I left Dana. Tashi had given birth. I sensed there was a parallel process with myself, yet to come. Tashi knew my hurts, body-wise, before I did. She also knew my emotional pain as well. Trying to revive my spirit one day, she invited me to join her in the upcoming visit by the Dalai Lama. Beginnings brought sadness and so I wasn't interested. However, once on the table, our conversation turned my feelings around and I decided to go, for I very much wanted to see this Holy Man. In fact, I then began to make a definite intention to get as close to him as I could.

He was to appear Memorial Day weekend at the inauguration of a Buddhist Temple in Kent, NY. Tashi called me the night before asking if I could give some friends of hers a lift. I quickly agreed awaiting yet another chance meeting. The newly found friends and I formed a caravan. The scenic route along the river proved restful and enjoyable. Once there, our group convened, anxiously awaiting his arrival. I needed to stretch my legs and so I walked around back of the beautiful temple. I saw a small crowd of people convening by a motor caravan. No photographers crowding around, no shouting or hysterical people; just quiet and humble people watching a man exit the limousine. It was the Dalai Lama. Feeling gratified just to get a glimpse of him, I ran back to the group. They were excited for me as well.

At the end of the ceremony, my newly introduced friends and I walked in and around the Temple. The temple is magnificent, with the largest statue of Buddha in the US. The grounds afforded a much needed contemplative atmosphere. Throngs of volunteers handed out gifts as we entered the grounds and afterwards served tasty and nutritious free meals. The love and generosity was contagious. As we walked around, we found a setting away from the crowd. The rock-like formations reminded us of an altar. It felt quite sacred. Once nestled in this setting, I was instantly reminded what a psychic said…that I would meet a man coming from a rock. I was to meet a very nice man that day. We spent the day together. However, nothing came of it, yet. I just noted it and let it go. We saw a box turtle hiding in the underbrush and we all petted him. His tiny head came out sensing a loving environment. What a special moment! After praying in the temple, we walked around to the back. We were interviewed by a reporter. Again, we saw His Holiness. Only this time, a few people, I being one of them, had our hands touched by Him. It happened so quickly that I don't recall seeing His face, only that tears came to my eyes. He quickly strode up a ramp to enter the temple, extending his hands to me, as well as others. What occurred next was magical. Strangers touched strangers faces, crying and caressing each other. It was an act of spontaneous Love, true Love. We were bathed in his energy of pure Love proving that Love IS and can be contagious!

I was truly blessed that day. And my hands, the hands that had been so cherished only a few days ago in the re-connecting ceremony, felt more than special. It felt as if it were an omen of blessings for this book.

CHAPTER ELEVEN: "THE LINEAGE DEEPENS"

On such a day as today, filled with alarming new information from my uncle about my mother, I am doubly pained by new information about my daughter. My mind is spinning. I had gone to my Uncle Peter's home to interview him earlier that day. I needed to get some history, for he's the only surviving member of the five siblings in my mother's family. I received a confirmation, as well as new piece to the puzzle. Either my mother or her sister had gone to Florida at sixteen. He felt it had something to do with an unborn baby. He doesn't know who said it. "Didn't I hear it from you, Elaine?" Always the projection.

A glimpse again into the Picchioni family. Three brothers, Paul, Peter and William or "Willi" as Grandma Rose used to say. Two sisters, my mother, called by several names Marguerite/Margherita or Margaret, and her beloved sister, Florence. Pete says Florence was the prettier of the two. And that my mother was very smart. According to my uncle, their father, the same man my mother revered, used to beat them as they ran around the dining room table naked. He'd use a clothesline tied in two. Grandfather had a brother, Cesare, in the US, whom Pete was very fond of. My uncle recalled how Cesare would give them candy. Cesare later returned to Italy, living in a house with animals, no screens, no doors. He later wound up in jail in Italy for molesting his kids. This, my grandfather's brother. Who were human, who were animals?

So now we see a different picture from the animated eighty-six year old woman in the rocking chair, in speaking of her happy childhood days. And to digest and integrate the two is no easy task. My grandfather would make wine in their home in North Bergen, NJ. They had chickens, pigeons and a goat for their milk and various vegetables in his garden. A picture emerges of a man of the land. Perhaps a savage, perhaps a rescuer, perhaps an intellectual. Perhaps a Jack, perhaps a Ralph, perhaps a Piggy. We shall never know the answer to the "perhaps." It is better that way. My grandmother, whom I never met, was a homemaker. In her autobiography, Mom would say "she was a good pie maker." They'd all have chores to do. Peter's was to take care of the animals. He recalls "things got better when his father remarried." Grandfather asked their permission to do so and the children were happy to have a mother again.

My memories contained none of the above events. But I have very precious and happy ones of my step-grandmother, "Grandma Rose" we used to call her. Grandma Rose was a saint. She treated my brother and I as cherished grandchildren praising and giving us candy and spoiling us like no other. To this day I cherish Grandma Rose's beautiful coral cameo pinky ring given to her when she was a servant in Chicago from an Italian family she cleaned house for. Later on it went to my mother and then myself. Lineage.

A mother cries out again to her daughter at the pond. A word of caution to a five year old. I cry out but am not heard. My daughter is thirty five-years old. She needs to learn caution on her own. I can no longer do that for her. I wish I could. Lisa is my eldest. Our entire family, though my husband and I are divorced celebrated her new, and hard won triumph as a journalist in Thibodeaux, Louisiana. Soon after my son Andrew's wedding, she called me up and said "Hi, Mom, are you sitting down?" "Lisa, whatever you have to say to me say it quickly without discussion. I know it's something that I won't like." I was right.

After living in Queens for ten years, Lisa left for Louisiana two weeks later. I was devastated. I again recall her question to me long ago when she was going away to college. "What can I do well, Mom?" Recalling her creative talent in art, needlepoint and writing, I quickly replied "Writing." After many jobs and much hard work, she has come into her own. She found her niche in journalism. She left New York recently to move to Louisiana. I miss her terribly.

Writing seems to be both contagious and running in our family for I told my mother that I had started my autobiography. She was quiet. Soon after, she announced she was writing a book. I smiled to myself - ever the competitive spirit. My brother found it in her belongings. What will my children find in my belongings that will be comforting to them? Once my mother died, I took the time to hurriedly read it as if I were wanting to avoid the painful passages. There were some. But what also was there was a detailed and exacting compilation of the deaths and births of three generations. I cherish that as well, though there were few emotional passages, mostly dates and a sentence or two saying "God Rest Your Soul." I can't bear to read these words again. Someday... I needed and yearned for some connection with her, once gone. One cannot hear a parent or see them as a person until they're dead. I know because this is happening to me now. And the pain is a festering, excruciating sore, especially on the day I found out about pain in my mother's family.

My mother and I would always visit at the same rendezvous in the front parlor of her home. She'd sit by the big picture window with her remote, puzzles, glasses, pens, pencils and the litany of pills by her side. I imagine the pills could be of some comfort to her. She didn't have much else but her illnesses. I spoke of Lisa who had told me she was being flown up to Connecticut for a job interview. I'm always happy to see my children usually forgetting the unpleasantness that it brings. I hadn't seen her since Christmas. It is now April. Where does the time go? Lisa flew in and out of New York without seeing me. Oh, the pain! When does it end? What happened to my five year old baby whom I used to nurture and love as best I could? Why this sudden callousness towards me? Why the divisiveness of mother/father. The marriage was long since over. Why the continued battle? Surely, I know the answer. Sameness at any cost, usually mine.

I received a call, then another from my ex-husband the day she flew in. None to me. It hurt. The hurt turned to anger and then disconnection. The same thing would happen when my children were younger. My parents treated them as if they were their children, not mine. It still enrages me. Lisa called the next day from Louisiana. By this time, it was too late. Lisa flew in and out of New York without ever seeing me.

CHAPTER TWELVE: "LOSS OF INNOCENCE"

This evilness, pain and distortions exist in all families. So it isn't surprising that the animated eighty-five year old woman had such fond memories of her childhood. Those were the best years of her life. Those were the years of innocence until innocence, almost necessarily so, was lost.

The trees are blooming. The blossoms appear as frothy pink and white cotton candy one buys at carnivals. The sweet sounds of birds chirping is an innocent sound. I adore that sound. It is one I am most familiar with, the same sound as my bird, Vita. My body was pulsing with creativity on the drive home from Elide's. We met at her apartment, overlooking Manhattan, with all their "penises," a term she fondly called skyscrapers. We discussed her book and I had so much energy that she urged me to return home and write.

The tape recorder was playing recently retrieved history from that days visit with my Uncle. "I'm flying free" were my thoughts as I drove up the Parkway feeling free as a bird. I felt joyful. My body pounding with newly surging energy. I was percolating! I approached a sharp curve in the road, driving a little too fast for the turn. Two birds suddenly appeared. I noted how playful and joyful they were. But not for long. Their dancing playful innocence was lost in a split second! The birds were gaily flying, but too low. My car swiftly maneuvered the sharp bend. The birds were midway between life and death. However, for one of them, there was no way out. The starling quickly dashed into the grill, blood spurting, feathers flying and disappeared. With sickness in my heart and stomach, I hoped, a futile hope, that the starling had survived. Unfortunately, he, or she, did not. The starling's companion flew overhead feverishly as if it too were dazed by the sudden loss.

Stopping the car brought me back to reality from futile wishes which were quickly dashed, as quickly extinguished as the starling's last joyful flight. I said a prayer and went to it. Its eyes were open. Except for a small pool of blood, its limp body was intact. Its tiny heart stopped. The little claws frozen in a futile grasp on life. The same kind of grasp my mother and I had in our hands. Life no more for mother, for bird.

The story I heard from my uncle was similar. Whether it be my aunt or my mother, what must have it been like to become motherless at ten years old, orphaned at twelve, and pregnant at sixteen? On a first date. Who did she turn to? What comfort could she have gotten? So alone.

The waters at Hook Mountain are choppy today. The river is churning with energy. Some people notice, others going about their lives, couples arm in arm, children feeding the ducks and seagulls, old men gathering to talk to each other - passing their remaining lives in nature. Seagulls flying high. Don't fly too high for your wings may melt and down you'll come, succumbing to the sea! "Stay close, close to your parents, don't leave!" Words, how well I remember those words, spoken and unspoken my entire lifetime. I tried to leave. I never did.

The starling's death deeply troubled me as I am driving to my massage appointment. What could it mean? Tashi offers some comfort. She informed me that in Tibetan culture, when an animal wishes to reincarnate as a human, it is necessary for it to be killed by a human in order to be born again. It lessened the pain somewhat but I still grieved and puzzled by the event. Agony quickly replaced the wonderful, energetic feeling of just a few hours ago.

"As suddenly as my mother lost both her parents," I thought. For she had gone to school both times when her parents had been killed, to return home without ever seeing them alive again. In the bird's death, I had a glimpse of my mother's pain certainly far greater than mine could ever be. What must it have been like to lose both parents within two years of each other? Orphaned! Alone! How horrible! How unimaginable! I returned home deep in sorrow, sorrow for the bird, sorrow for my mother's pain, and sorrow for the lost precious moments of the joyful part of that day.

I began to sculpt with clay. A bird appeared with large, pronounced, majestic wings. I recognized it as the bird that had died. I became impatient as it wasn't turning out to my liking, and so I stopped and decided instead to meditate, seeking solace at my altar. The energy was still coursing through me, like a steady stream of water; the sign of another message about to come through.

With palms facing upward in a receiving gesture, energy coursing through my body, especially my hands, I surrendered to silence and the moment. Breathing deeply and smoothly, my eyes began to sink deeper into their sockets. I expectantly awaited the unknown. My eyes were closed but a minute when I suddenly had a vision of the bird, the very same bird! However, now its wings, black and speckled were outstretched in a huge wingspan that reminded me of an eagle. This starling with wings outstretched was upright as if it had already been resurrected. It looked incredibly alive, alert, and happy. As I kept pace with my breathing and the vision, I saw an infant emerge from the starling's body. I was surprised by my own image! Though deep in the meditative process, still connected with the vision, my mind wandered to another image. It was of a painting I'd seen of a shaman. Shaman's body and head were ensconced in an eagle's body.

The message was signaling rebirth, though when and what form was still unclear. The infant began to meld into a white flying horse! Pegasus! My mind was battling my senses and experience. Words became audible. Someone was talking to me. "I am Icarus, your guide." OK! But Icarus drowned when his waxed wings flew too close to the Sun. Icarus was seeking freedom. His wings melted and HE was enveloped by the sea! Similar to my fear for the seagulls at Hook Mountain! "No!," I said. "I don't want you as my guide!" I was instructed not to tell anyone. That didn't feel right and I was mistrustful at that point. I didn't want to contend with and be distracted by guides that would talk to me all the time. And so I tuned it out. But not the message.

The message was clear. Balance is necessary. Don't fly too high or you'll be killed like the bird. But there is a more important message. One, that we are all protected by invisible forces; guides, if you wish. I prefer to think of it as the Holy Spirit. The other message, most importantly, was of the cycle of rebirth. My rebirth was symbolically proclaimed. I AM A SHAMAN! I now have wings to fly, with caution and discretion.

I'm looking at the seagulls again. They hover overhead and then fly down for food. Food is in the water not up in the air. Message received. Aptly and humbly integrated. Innocence lost and then Rebirth. Is that why addictions are so tempting? An attempt to "fly high" like the bird to freedom. Freedom of their youth. Freedom to simpler, better days.

My mother's body continues the imagined comforting momentum of her rocking chair my father bought for her at eighty-five, smiling her impish, devilish smile, still telling her childhood stories...real...or imagined?

CHAPTER THIRTEEN: "DEATH NOT QUITE YET"

It is very painful to write of my mother,. Her innocence was lost many times, which seemed to follow her into adulthood and marriage with several abortions. Her interest in becoming a teacher was affected by those losses, and she told me that at some point she didn't like children anymore except those very close to her in her family. Another death. I now understand why. So sad I couldn't have asked her when she was alive the questions that are only speculations now. I am sure fear kept her locked into herself.

As I look at the river now I am suddenly struck by the ambiguities. A train is spiraling up the river, its silver bullet swiftness in command. A downward spiral is also occurring with the river's southerly direction. Is that how she must have felt when her innocence was lost? Is that why the rocking chair was flying freer and faster than her little body and little feet, could carry it? The body's animation was like the five year old facing the pond the other day. The mother was cautioning the child to go slow. Is that the way my mother protected me from the world? Holding onto me meant holding onto life's innocence? But it didn't work. It never does. It's not meant to!

We need the innocence and we need it to be lost in order to come to wholeness. The child grows up soaring high and wanting to be free as the bird. And to be born again out of the womb of the bird, as in meditation after the starling's "accidental" and very unexpected demise the other day. But my mother and many like her didn't know HOW! This might have been her unconscious wish. To unite with another. To give birth to life. To make up for the two lives that suddenly died. How wonderful. How sad. "No judgment taken, Mom."

Two years ago, I was awakened at 3AM with a phone call from my father. "Your mother is sick. She has to go to the hospital." Familiar and dreaded words. The dread that is in all of our hearts. I stumbled for my balance, reeling in shock. Throwing on clothes, my mind soared as fast as the racing car. Will she be OK? Will she die? I then knew the reason she hadn't been calling me recently. Thoughts went to our last visit. It was the summer of 1994.

E coli was in the news. E coli was in my mother's mind. She felt it was in her body. It may have been. She had been self medicating and the laxatives had depleted her system of salt. She was psychotic and speaking only of "E Coli" when I saw her last. I was trying to live my own full life and be a good daughter as well. The resentment came out in that visit. I wasn't compassionate. We spoke across the kitchen table. Mother sitting in her usual chair by the stove. I sitting in my Father's chair by the back door to the porch. The window between us, seemed to be metaphoric as well; separating two females from different eras. We were two strangers; one separated from the womb; the other from shame and guilt, lies and cover-ups. As I think about it now, it seemed all so pointless.

She was picking at her arms as she usually did. She hated those scabs and tried to remove them. "Don't pick them," I said. I could have said "Why do you pick them? What's wrong, Mom?" I didn't. I couldn't. My ears and heart were closed. They had been open for too long. They hurt. My hurt. My mother's hurt. Closed eyes, ears, heart, and a dead soul or souls? Unborn souls.

Logistically, we could no longer transport her to the hospital where my father had worked as a chef. Nor the same hospital my brother studied medicine in. No longer could she have her favorite doctor. She had to go to the nearest hospital; ironically the same hospital I had worked at as a social worker. At this point, time was of the essence. All I could do was say a prayer and trust she would get the help she needed. It was out of my control. Life's funny that way. It has the controls. I welcomed the surrender.

My mother spent ten long hours in the emergency room. Her frail, bony body lay on a gurney in a hallway, and on a bed pan for most of that time. The indignity of it all. The irony of it all. Lying in a corridor in the same hospital I had recently left…left to fulfill my own life. Leaving the Bronx, meant leaving my parents. A necessary leaving. Innocence lost. Freedom gained. If one has the right key to the door.

My mind was spinning. Is this real? Is this happening? Again! So many agains! My mother had been in hospitals most of her adult life. She had many ailments. She suffered greatly and always quietly. She was a "good girl patient." Women have to be good. So good.

Don't speak. Don't say what hurts you. Be silent. Just take it out on your body and your soul. "That's a good girl."

The stay there was to be for a long, hard month. My mother required round the clock private nursing in the beginning. She was strapped to the bed. Her arm again came out of the socket. Again she had to have it reset. She was to have it set one more time…when she was in her final death throes. "Oh, dear God," I thought, "just let her rest in peace!"

The daughter in the woman in me was screaming inwardly. Always taking care of her. When would it be my turn? I chose carefully time spent with her during that stay, for I had recently left the Bronx to further my career and personal development. It was a necessary leaving. It was time. I had completed most of my work in the eight years I was at the hospital. I repeatedly asked my parents if they'd missed me. Not a word was said, more silence to cover up hurts and a body to contain it. It just was. "Was" was deposited in the body, the mind, the heart, the soul. That's where the "was" goes. The deposit eats at the body. I know. I receive and believe in healing bodywork. Body work is a necessary element to me for energy and breath is all we really have.

The month-long stay bought her a vacation. The month long stay brought one caring and nurturing. Her husband did both. She just needed a new environment. Women in "those days" didn't know where to go for the "new environment." Most went to hospitals or to drugs, or to depression, or just died. This was the Italian woman's heritage, welcomed or not. It just was…and is?????

The arm reset, strapped to the bed, she remained a "good patient." Quietly, with her large eyes, my mother silently looked at the drama and many dramas, in the four-bed ward as life unfolded before those eyes - the keys to her freedom. Eyes! I wince now. I cry now for her pain. I light a candle now. I bring her last photograph to comfort both she and I. I place it on top of the computer, so fraught with meaning, that I purchased from my lover. I light a candle and incense. She is with me. I love her. I wish I told her more! Life is funny that way, isn't it? At once, I hear my shaman friend's voice. "Stay conscious." Staying conscious would have brought more hugs, more tears, more joy, more realness. Staying conscious first brings more pain and THEN the joy!

My mother would lay on a stretcher waiting for this, that or another test. The portrayal now is not of the critical, insensitive parent. The portrayal is of the frail, vulnerable, aging woman in pain underneath her crusty disguise. My heart went out to her. I was able to love her. "Mom, when you get home, and that sling is off your arm, you're going to give me a big hug. And I'm going to give you one back!" Why do we have to wait? Always waiting. Never comes. Love never waits. It is always there.

The Angels took care of her stead, as they must now be doing wherever she is resting. There was one in particular at the hospital. My mother was in a ward with four women. She'd sit up, strapped in bed, arm in a sling, quietly observing the "circus" atmosphere. Her keen eyes took it all in. There wasn't anything she'd miss.

There was Diane, a heavyset woman with a serious heart ailment. You'd never know it from her hearty, joyful demeanor. She loved my mother. I love her for that. I never called her to say my mother had died. Perhaps there's a part of me that can't or won't acknowledge her death. Diane would tell jokes with the sardonic sense of humor that only another ill person could appreciate. I know. I recall meeting a man who was to have one of the first heart transplants when he and I were patients in the '60's. He never made it. Diane was hilarious. The other two women, including my mother, were fodder for her antics. One day she told me that my mother had almost fell, inches away from disaster. Somehow she had slid out of the chair she was strapped into. An aide, passing by in the hall saw what was happening and quickly rushed to her bedside. Her Angel, who saved her for us for two more years.

The nurse that took care of mom wasn't a stranger to me. She and I would often trade jokes at lunchtime outside the hospital. She would saunter over to the owner's truck, and start taking food orders. We'd often joke that he made the best greasy sandwiches cholesterol ever had. Her sense of humor equaled her apt abilities as a nurse. I recall the day we picked up my mother from the hospital. She was emaciated. A pathetic, boney, figure. That same nurse was inserting a catheter. One of the other indignities that my mom had endured in silence. "Does she have to have that?" I inquired. Trying to hold my anger down, but not in. "Yes, you know your mother has a bladder problem," and, I thought to myself, "a heart and soul problem as well!" Always the tending to the body not the soul. "OK" I said, knowing full well it would be out in a few hours by either my brother or sister-in-law, both doctors.

My father was waiting in the car. "You go and get her" said he. The "good girl" went and got my mother. She could hardly climb into the car. I had to lift up her legs. Once in, the body remained in one fixed place. No energy to be comfortable. Just be as it was. The two steps to what would be her home for the next two years, were almost insurmountable. Quietly she dragged her tired legs, her tired body up them. She could not make the stairs to her bed.

That was the beginning of the end; the end of her sickness, the end of her life. The journey home to her Creator had begun. As a testimony to her tenacity, and to the family's surprise and gratitude, Mom began to blossom in her remaining years. Even her later photos show her soul work, for as a younger woman she never wanted her picture taken. She never looked good in them. Now, Mom's last treasured picture looks at me. She has her angel pin on top of the picture. There is a family walking by my window as I write this. I envy them.

CHAPTER FOURTEEN: "THE BURIAL"

The bird's death had meaning beyond the conscious mind. Feeling the need to ritualize, sacredize and respect this tiny creature, I buried its lifeless body. I placed a red carnation on its breast and laid it to rest underneath my apartment window. No sooner had I left, that a scavenger upset my plan. Perhaps, I thought, I need to let nature take its course. Controls wouldn't allow me to do that. And so I took it up to my apartment terrace, placed it reverently in a secure temporary grave site and pondered the new event.

The burial of the bird reminded me of my mother's burial. A painful, raw memory of a year ago... I had decided once I got back from visiting my Shaman friend in Philadelphia, that I needed to go away for a retreat. However, before doing so, I drove to visit my parents. They never liked it when I vacationed. I was leaving them again; going away. Abandonment issues, theirs, and perhaps mine as well, would open oozing, untreated wounds of the past. "One never knows," I thought. "Just in case."

No sooner did I get there that my father and I were arguing as we had during my teen years. This time about where I should park the car. My emotions were raw and rage filled. It was as abhorrent then, as now. Looking back, I believe it was part of the Divine Plan, for it all seemed unusual, and uniquely planned.

After what seemed like an interminable amount of time, and energy, I entered the house, walked through the double set of French doors in the long narrow, hallway that contained memories of mother's family, and saw my mother in the corner of the living room. Before going to her, I stepped on the small runner by the French door. The same runner that still reeks of my mother's spilt blood and last passion. In effect, the runner contains my mother's grave site. That is where she fell the night of the lunar eclipse in 1996.

The small green runner was there to wipe one's feet on before coming into the livingroom and/or dining room. Father, in his perpetual comings and goings from one entranceway to another, would trek in mud, driving my neat and orderly mother crazy. The living room reeked of Italianesque icons. A gold wooden Florentine clock on the wall over the TV. The many pictures underneath the TV stand of grandchildren in various stages of their growth. The falling down, plop on couch the grandchildren, young and old, loved to lie on. Invariably they would fall asleep watching the TV that constantly droned during their visits. The cocktail table with an always filled up candy jar; the words "For My Favorite Grandchildren" emblazoned on it. The Italianesque leather carved table lamps from the 1950's. The lamps, an inexpensive copy of ones my mother admired from my home. The books underneath the long cocktail table that contained medical data…a gift from her son, "the Doctor!"

The only new addition in the forty-three years they lived in the house was the recliner, and the pretty oriental green flowered area rugs my brother purchased for them for their 60th wedding anniversary. New items only came into the house for special events; otherwise everything went to their children and grandchildren - rarely for themselves. "Old" items went to hospitals, or funeral homes, and graves.

I walked towards her, my father following, still shouting at me. The argument continued, commanding and riveting my attention with my mother the silent witness. I barely glanced at my mother but enough to notice that she looked frailer than usual. She was very quiet, wearing the signs of her generation—an apron, and a weary smile. She wasn't sitting in her new rocking chair but in Dad's gold velvet recliner set in the corner of the living room, with the old fashioned upright lamp behind it.

My father's anger emanated from his wanting me to take care of his wife. My life needed to go on. HE needed to take care of HIS wife. I had done so for too many years. My mother was quiet. I didn't even sit down and talk to her. I just went to her and said "I love you," kissed her for what was to be the last time and left. Before doing so, I said to him, "And I'm not calling." And I didn't. My mother said, "But Sunday is Palm Sunday."…as if she were trying, one last time to hold onto me…to not go…to not leave her…If only. "Yes, Mom, I know. I'm going to get you some palms." They were in her room when she died. There is another one waiting in my care, and car, for my father. It was incredible. This last family triangular drama was set up this way. Sort of like "jetti- songing" her to Heaven because of the immense bond the three of us have.

I didn't call home. Instead I received a knock on the door at 11:30 PM, "to call Barbara." As I walked down the three flights of stairs to the phone, I wondered why my colleague Barbara was calling at this time of night. Denial had time to set in. My mind was wandering back to the events of the day. I had watched a video of Buddhist monk, Thich Nacht Han, who spoke about forgiveness. He spoke about parents, anger and a wonderful method of forgiving the hurt. His words were spoken simply and with a truism that went to my heart. Afterwards, with tears in my eyes, I felt the need to go to the Meditation Room. Once there, I deeply prostrated my body in a most humble prayer position. Sobbing profusely, I cried out "I don't know why I'm crying but I know it is for something very important." At that same time, my mother got up from her recliner, hurriedly ran towards the dining room, falling face first on the green runner. The scent of her spilt blood is still with us today; the blood spilt for her and her family.

The day my mother fell was an unusually calm and peaceful day for me. I was at Kripalu, a holistic, world renowned yoga retreat center. I go there to re-connect, to re-energize heart and soul when I hurt. Kripalu is a wonderful, high energy place. The year was 1996. The month April. There was a lunar eclipse that evening.

I wandered into the cafeteria, met an artist from Woodstock and had a long and connected conversation. At 8pm, we stopped chattering and went outside to view the eclipse. The sky was clear. The stars were shining. In the eerie and beautiful darkness, we watched as nature showed her resplendence to her children. But her children were chattering, grounded in the crisp, cold, clear air of the wonderful Berkshire Mountains. We hurried back into the warmth of the building unaware of the last life drama of my beloved mother.

I went to bed around 10pm. I was innocent of events to come. Innocent in mind, but the body knew. The conversation with a massage therapist during the video came back to me. What was the meaning of our connection? I would soon find out. Though the day was quiet, my body and mind were restless that night. I tossed and turned in my bed. "Must be the eclipse," I thought. I couldn't sleep. Then, the eternal and universal feared knock on the door. The registrar in his bathrobe apologized for waking me. He left me a telephone number to call. "Barbara? What's Barbara doing calling me at this time?" I hadn't been in touch with her since our days together on the psychiatric unit at the hospital." I was innocent during the long walk down three flights of stairs.

News of my mother's fate was given a few minutes reprieve. The dimly lit corridors allowed me a temporary pardon from grief. However, when I reached the phones, the bright lights lit up the area code and telephone number. My legs shook. My body shivered. It was my sister-in-law, Barbara! How quickly the body summons up denial at a time like this. I dialed the number. Barbara answered. "She fell". I immediately knew who "she" is, or was? My body still, heart pounding, lips and ears acutely aware of its tasks, I waited. "Gerry is on his way there. She's in a coma." I swiftly replied, "I'm on my way." Though it was late at night, the massage therapist was suddenly by my side. "Could you please let the desk clerk know that I'm leaving?" An angel sent. Connection now understood. Hurriedly, and with heavy heart, but with determination and steel-like complacency of mind, I rushed to pack. Everything was done with silent, sudden strength and intention.

The sky was now lit up by the full moon. It was midnight. I solemnly went to my car, feeling very alone. "Shit, no gas." At a time like this! I drove the darkened, strange highway hoping to find a gas station. To fill the gap in the heart hole, I played the "Chant" tape over and over again. That somber music is forever etched in memory. The repetition was soothing to the heart. Tears could not come. I drove slowly. The road, the seemingly endless road, appeared to be getting darker. Finally, I saw light, a store. A kind policeman pumped the gas. He knew, silently, from my state of being. Another angel sent to me. When I went inside to pay, the woman at the counter in the all-night "convenience" store gave me a hard time about nonsense. I again uttered the feared words of every child, "My mother is dying. I need to go!"

I slowly steeled myself for what I now knew was the inevitable. My mother WAS indeed dying! This is it. I couldn't escape the inevitable, and so I prayed for her and for myself. I drove slowly, stopping only to call my brother on her condition. I needed the time to collect myself. I arrived at the hospital at 3:30am - the same time as two years ago. Same time, different hospital, same patient. "She" was indeed in a coma. I now knew why my body was so tired these many months. I knew, as I know my own name, that I was carrying in my body her passion. Only the words couldn't or didn't come out. A year ago, after waking up from a dream the words "My mother was leaving," were also preparing me for her demise. The same as in the Valentine's Day meditation. I'm not alone.

Her shoulder had to be reset, for the last time, from the fall. Something to do with the circulation. She was having a heart attack. Her arm again in a sling, was totally black from the fall. Her eyes had huge circles around them, similar to a racoon. Her breathing labored, her eyes closed. She was on life support systems. Not for long. I held her hand. I spoke to her, words that one speaks to a dying person. That I loved her. That I hadn't meant to leave her. I kissed her. I wept. I covered her cold, diabetic feet with socks. The next day at the river's edge I saw a huge cloud of a perfect foot. Signs. Comfort. When one needs it most.

The routine of going in and out of her room was also comforting. It was very quiet. Nurses were attending to her. There was dignity here; this, her last final visit to the last final hospital bed. To the last final hospital stay. The last final "vacation." She was going home at last! Her husband, who so devotedly cared for her, was back home. Home was what was good for him for he was ninety. "She" had been bleeding profusely from the fall for an hour. Lying face down in her blood, "she" still gave orders to her husband and the kind neighbor, a nurse from next door. "She" didn't want to go to the public hospital "she" had been in only two years prior. "She" waited the long torturous hour for an ambulance to a private hospital. Father going and doing, in dying, as he had done in life, caring for her as her obedient and faithful servant. When "she" got to the hospital, her last words, to the doctor were "Put me in a box" and "she" went into a coma. "She" was ready. As I write this, it feels uniquely ordained. She had her final goodbyes to her beloved husband and beloved home. Her goodbyes to her children were from her deathbed.

My mother died on Holy Thursday, fell on the first day of Passover and was buried on Palm Sunday with the palms I had promised her in life, now in her casket, on her way to new life. She covered all the bases. It was a tribute to her last passion to die during Jesus' Last Passion. The starling rests outside my bedroom window. I know it is there; a marker of sacrifice. My mother rests in New Jersey. I have her with me, in me and through me; forever, in my heart, in my soul, in my presence, in my essence. Daughter to mother. Woman to woman. Blood to blood.

The funeral was the only funny thing in this sad life drama. The funeral home people were cold blooded mafiosos. They hurried my father along, up the many steps to the church. I will never forgive them for that. But we had the last laugh my brother and I; tricksters that we are. Feigning biological urges, I asked the driver to stop the hearse "one last time" by her home. "Let them wait," I said as my brother and I got out of the car giggling as if we were adolescents. I was angry at their insensitivities. Later, my ever-discreet brother shocked me when he asked the driver what part of the Mafia operated in this area. We sank down in our seats at that remark. It seemed as if we got to New Jersey by way of China, as they were so used to escape routes, that we took all the back roads! We were hysterical at the sign by the entrance to the cemetery; "Tombstone Bar & Grill." We all needed the macabre humor! My brother even took pictures of my mother in her casket. Bizarre as it was, it was a sense of comfort to me. He also took wonderful snapshots of the setting sun that day. Memories.

My son and his family came to the hospital early the day of my mother's death. My brother and I were there at the very end, alone with our mother. It was 3:20pm this time. Gerald said my mother was going fast. I rushed out the door leaving him alone with our mother. I had made a snap decision that he needed that. If she died before I returned, I would be at peace with my decision. Mother and I had made our peace. Our relationship had healed over these last two years. He needed that gift. They both did.

I wanted to find a candle so we could wish her "Happy Birthday" into the next and new life. A life without pain. A life without suffering. A life with as much reason and purpose as this one and, I am sure, a life rewarded for the suffering and sacrifices she made in this one. I went about this with similar determination as when I drove to her the night of the full moon. Quiet, intentionally, prayerfully and reverently. The women scattered for candles. "None here, sorry," said the many people the secretary phoned. I remained silent and patient. I knew they would appear. All of a sudden I had one candle, then two, then three. More than I needed. I rushed to my mother's side. Just in time. "Hurry, she's going" said my brother. I lit the

70

candle. My brother and a nurse were at her side. The picture of my mother above her head. The window blinds we had quickly rolled up, shone light in this sterile environ and on her failing body.

"Happy Birthday, Mom, Godspeed." Silently, ever so silently, still, quietly, she surrendered - to Life!

CHAPTER FIFTEEN: "LIFE"

The burial of my mother created a new beginning in me. Before her death, I had slowly and steadily been separating. However, I wasn't prepared for the final separation, and its' concurrent raising of strange, and empty feelings. I felt TOTALLY disconnected. The emptiness was confusing, and unbearable at the same time. Her earthly life was gone; as mine began to carve out a new beginning. Grief now no longer yearned for separateness, but rather for a material connection that was not possible. A spiritual connectedness didn't seem possible as well, for my anger was in the way. I had waited so very long for my freedom, and I still blamed her for my not acquiring it sooner. The grieving process was in full swing and I needed to flounder in it for as long as necessary. I still hadn't reclaimed my self, only I didn't know it at the time.

When I hear the word "life" I think about beginnings. Beginnings of both my life and my mother's. Another female, my first granddaughter, Amanda, was born five months after my mother's death. Born in September, the same month as my mother - a Virgo. The virgin. Critical, cynical, that was my mother. She'd say "So what!" as often as she'd breathe. Everything had dismissal, even her self, especially her body.

I pondered questions: "Who was the 'baby that died before me' so I could write this book?" And the intuition that I have a sister still alive? What does it all mean?" Several psychics have confirmed what a psychic had said fifteen years ago. She's still alive. She was "handed over." No other information other than her name is/was Cynthia/ Stephanie. Time will unfold the rest at will. Perhaps I'm not ready to accept a sister at this point, and perhaps I'm protecting her for she's around seventy-three years old and it might be a shock to her. Till then, I knew I needed to reclaim my life more than my sister's life!

In order to do that, I began again, by looking back to my earlier roots. I'm the eldest of two children born to Marguerite and Gerolamo Cordani, an only child for seven long years until my brother arrived. I have few memories. But I do recall how I first heard of my brother's impending birth - from my Aunt Carrie, perhaps because birth had such a loaded meaning for my mother. I cried and cried in our small living room. I don't recall where my mother was at the time but my aunt and I were in the apartment. My mother's pregnancy is a total blur. It was as if I wasn't a part of it, feeling separated and disconnected then. When my parents came home with Gerald or "Jiggy" for short, he was crying. I went to his crib in my parent's bedroom, and handed him a handkerchief to blow his nose! Oh, how I feel such tenderness for my lonely little child having to intuitively take on a maternal role much earlier than necessary. My brother was as much a stranger to me as I was to myself. We lived separate lives in the same family. It was as if seven years was an eternity that one could not surpass.

Our family lived in a Bronx apartment house on the third floor, right next to the elevator that I'd hear droning during the night. I'd hear it because I slept in the nearby living room which would be my bedroom for sixteen long years till I graduated from high school. Our apartment consisted of three small rooms. One would walk in the front door with a long hallway to the living room. To the right was the kitchen, which had interesting "things" that most apartments might not have today. There was a large old fashioned sink, a stove that just served, like my mother. There was an old metal, enamel green and black kitchen table. To the left, almost as if it foretold of the importance food was in our family, setting all by itself, was "The" refrigerator. Its' freezer compartment conjures up memories of homemade ice cream Mom and I would make and freeze in the ice cube trays. I enjoyed waiting expectantly for the ice cream to freeze so we could eat it. There were cabinets above and alongside the refrigerator. I especially recall the ones above for two reasons: one, Mom and I would take down and wash all the dishes once a year, and two, on Sunday mornings my father would retrieve a glass and make zabaglione for me. I can still taste the sweetness of the sugar, egg and vermouth concoction. But most of all, I recall his caring. The stove conjures up images of making pizza for my mother when she was sick. I was so proud of myself at how it came out for it wasn't often that I had a sense of mastery in my childhood days. To the right of the repository for THE refrigerator is a window. My window to "the world". My small world. The window faced a courtyard separating two large apartment buildings. Directly across the courtyard lived another family whom I'd watch when I couldn't sleep at night.

Underneath the window was an "ice box" a non-refrigerated cold storage area that my father would keep his gallon of wine in. I recall sitting at the kitchen table in the corner by the "dumb waiter" on a green and black wooden chair. What an interesting name. Dumb waiter! I suppose because "it" also never talked, just served, like my mother. I'd either do my homework there while munching on food, or in the bedroom. Many a day was spent looking out the window at the myriad of apartments facing us. I'd gaze in the windows seeing unknown faces and bodies walking to and fro wondering what life was like for them. My fertile imagination would churn out fantasies. "Are they happy? Sad? What do they do in their family setting?" I'd notice when curtains were changed, season-wise. I also heard loud laughter as well as arguments. I'd pine and yearn for unknown needs and wants that I wasn't yet connected to. That would come much later.

The next room off the hallway was the living room. There was a patterned pink, yellow and green linoleum covering the floor. Carpeting was a rarity in those days. There were two windows in the room. Several pieces of furniture come to mind...a couch along the left wall, the green chair by the window, and a combination radio and tv set in the corner which is now in my brother's old room. In the left hand corner was a closet; the closet I'd store my clothes in, as well as use for a dressing room. In the winter, the closet was nice and warm and comforting. That same corner was the sole niche that held my small, private space. I slept on a cot or "branda" in Italian. It would be my bed for sixteen years. I recall the heavy damask pink fabric that rested in that corner. The drapes on the windows matched the pink brocade fabric. I felt a sense of loss when my father gave the "branda" and covering to the next door neighbor.

I graduated at some point to the green single convertible chair bed near the window around teen years purchased for my uncle's brief stay with us, a stay and reasons I cannot recall. The most vivid scene of the green chairbed was sitting on it one day, feeling quite sick and wondering what this "bloody stuff" was oozing out of me. My mother harshly said "That's your period. Get used to it." Comforting words, defensive words, now understandable words - to hide her "getting used too's" - too many tragedies to offer comfort to others, as none were given to her.

The "branda" would be put away during the day, covered and silent, and rolled out and opened at night. Night time was my secret and quiet time. I'd read science fiction stories until my mother roared from her bedroom "Shut the light out and get to sleep." That's when I resorted to a flashlight. I learned to be very resourceful, secretive and creative in my small space. Off the living room was a small hallway that led to my parents and brother's bedroom. There was a small bathroom to the right. On the wall opposite the bathroom was a phone; not just our phone but a shared phone called a "party line." If one picked up the phone and the other party was on, it certain wasn't a "party" trying to get them to hang up. The phone brings back memories of a gang of kids going across the street to the train station to make prank phone calls; those rites of passages of adolescents.

There were two windows in the bedroom. One window had a fire escape that either went up the remaining three stories or down two to ground level. That was the sole "air conditioner" in the house. During the summer one either sat out on the fire escape, went up to the roof, called "tar beach," or out front where one would fight to get a seat on "the stoop." I remember my parents' bedroom set. We still have the dresser in my father's attic. It has burled inlaid wood, curved legs and cascading drawers that lead to elegant, sturdy legs supporting it. It is difficult to say "father's attic" instead of my "parents' home." What will I say, what will it be like when my father dies? Whose home will it be then? Where will I take my emptiness?

The bedroom was a sore subject for me, for when the door closed, my mind opened to unlimited fantasies. I was alone, and felt left out. Once the school day ended, I'd ensconce myself on my parent's bed, stealing temporary ownership where there was none at night. I'd spend many a time there daydreaming. My brother's small crib was there, silently, but imposingly, in the corner along the bathroom wall.

Memories of bedrooms bring back homework and studying. I recall the days when our family doctor would go in that room to treat my mother. Mother seemed always to be ill but there never was a name for the sickness. My father would be there and the doctor, both solemn and quiet. There were no comforting words for my frightened young child. The silence was deafening and haunting then, as it is now. I was alone in a seeming chasm on the other end of the closed door, always fearing for my mother's life left to my fertile imagination, and unknowing silent rage.

The living room brings back memories of radio days and our first TV set. The Sunday night TV shows were eagerly awaited by the entire family. All of us would gather around the set, brother and I on the floor, parents on the couch. I have fond memories of those precious, and rare, family times together. Life was simple except for the air raids. The livingroom drapes, heavily weighted, would be hurriedly pulled shut, as would all the lights in the house. Is was then, I believe, fantasies of German blond men materialized into my imagination, and I subsequently married my fantasy.

The most vivid and hilarious memories of apartment living was when tv first came out. Only one family in the entire apartment complex had one. On Tuesday nights, most of the kids on the block would eagerly find the way to their fourth floor home. We'd excitedly run down the hall, and wait in excited anticipation as we rang the doorbell. Once inside, Milton Berle, as "Uncle Miltie," magically appeared on this wonderful new invention, in the "Texaco Hour." The show in the apartment with the antics of the couple's only child, was just as hilarious. He'd romp on the couch, jump on the furniture and invariably the harried mother would scream for her husband to stop him. That never happened. Meanwhile the kids, with row upon row of little heads and little bodies sat dazed and captivated by the mesmerizing images and roar with laughter at Milton Berle's antics, and by the images of the new "machine."

Oh, for those simple days again! Does the pain ever end? Do I have to retrieve my roots before I retrieve myself, I wonder? So many questions, so few answers, so little time.

CHAPTER SIXTEEN: "MOTHER'S DAY"

It is now two days till Mother's Day. Always a painful day for me, as I left my marriage, my children, my home, the week before Mother's Day. I'm in my car at Hook Mountain after an emotion-filled day's visit to my son's home. My car carries the remnants of today…an empty Taco Bell burrito wrapper, an unread manuscript, another rejection from one of my children who refused to read it, some new clothes to take the edge off the hurt, dirty white socks and sneakers for the walk around the lake to burn off steam - and new and old anger of memories and emotions of the past. The unfulilled yearnings for a functional and close family welled up in my body as I drove home.

Thank goodness, I had someone to talk to once leaving my son's home. I was meeting my friend, Samantha, for lunch afterwards. I cried out to her "Again it happened with my family! Again the hurt, anger and disappointment! When will I ever learn? I feel as if I've come full circle." That was to be the theme of our time together. Cycles. Indeed, it brought me back to when my son was four years old.

My son Andrew recently fell and broke his collarbone. The same one his father broke when he was four. Oh, the pain of seeing my son standing at the back door of the house I used to call home, his body clothed in a short green jumpsuit and striped red, white and green shirt. His tiny legs bare except for shoes and socks; his left arm hanging limp by his side. My heart went out to him, my anger raged at my husband. The pediatrician decided not to press charges. "It was an accident." An accident? Of sorts. But the ghosts remain to this day. Ghosts haunt families more than they know couched in either memories or repression.

I had seen my ex- husband just the day before. He called in response to my seeking some papers I needed, and may have left at "his" house. They were in his house, the house and home that I left some eleven years ago. The houses of all our family's minds are haunted by that leaving. It is time to let go.

Samantha and I spoke of cycles and circles today, a day suddenly bringing me back some twenty-nine years ago. My son's arm was broken when my ex-husband reprimanded him for throwing a large

77

rock at Lisa. The recent injury again caused chaos in our family. The pain reopened, the wound oozing old pus, silently shouting seething torments of yearned for healings.

Telephone game began. Andrew calls my brother, the doctor. My father calls me and tells me about My son. I call my son and tell him I'm hurt. My ex-husband hears it from me, calls my son, coming full circle with anger towards me! There is no sense and logic to it all; just repetitive unhealthy actions demanding health and growth.

Mother's Day is when I left my husband eleven years ago. I remember it well. I'd finally decided to divorce after many unfulfilled years. The children were grown and out of the house. I first told my youngest daughter Tracy and regret it to this day as it was the first night spent home from college for summer vacation and last semester before graduation. I left her and the house at the same time I left their father. I recall asking her later if it was better without the arguing. She said it was "quieter" but not "better". And certainly sadder? My middle child, Andrew, had to be found first as he was racing his motorbike. My daughter Lisa was very supportive. Both daughters helped me move. My son opposed the separation, saying "To death do you part." I couldn't wait that long. My belief, dissimilar to my parents' generation, is that when love ends, one needs to move on. That is not to say that I didn't try to fix the marriage. I tried to a fault. Some things can't be fixed. And like a precious, but fragile china cup that can't be mended has to be bravely let go of.

I dreaded Mother's Day for many reasons. My eldest hadn't called since she flew in and out of New York. My son was angry at me. "One out of three isn't bad..." as I said to my youngest. Walking wearily up the three flights of steps to my apartment I was greeted with the magnificence of a huge azalea plant. It was perfect timing, less timing than I had had in telling her of my separation decision eleven years ago. We had a wonderful talk on the phone. I treasure the way the relationship is slowly growing and building ever stronger than ever. I had just come back from lunch with Samantha. Rebuffed by my son and daughter-in-law saying "this has got to stop." "This" of course is The Ghost of the marriage. The failed marriage! Say it! Failed! But "how" and "why" did it happen,"I thought in my car coming home? The answer was right in front of me. Nature is devoid of Man's judgment, because of its' supreme power, as well as an example of God's act of resplendent creation. Man, however, is as frail as the china cup; and unlike nature, humans cannot accept another's imperfections!

That "how" brought me to my lover's place of business. I yearned to be with him, to be held, to cry in his arms. But I dared not be rebuffed again. The fear kept me locked inside my pain. I circled around his car, phoned home to see if he had called. No call. I went round and round, my heart aching till finally I was able to leave as I had left my marriage. Will I have the heart to leave him as well? Not easily though.

I traveled around the area I had worked in, aware of cycles again, as I thought back to the memories when I was a student. Very happy memories of meeting my lover and leaving my marriage. Lover, husband, son: these three factors - three most important men in my life next to my father and brother. The pain was unbearable. Incredibly, it almost hurt more than when I left the marriage. I couldn't sleep from physical and emotional pain. My shoulder pain, ever present from the accident, was now excruciating. Tossing and turning didn't help. I jumped out of bed and went to my sacred space, my altar. Again tucked away in a corner like my "branda" only this time much more elegant looking. The altar is behind a magnificent dark, hand-carved Indian screen, instead of a cot. I began to meditate, tears no longer held back. After the meditation still unable to sleep, I had breakfast ...at 2:30am!

Finally, weariness and oatmeal helped me succumb to sleep. I was awakened by Lisa wanting to make amends. I didn't hear love. I heard guilt. I heard what I used to say to my mother. I didn't really understand my mother's pain. I couldn't. It was too painful to hear. The same with my children. I spoke of my pain. The reply "Work through the pain." "You're still my mother but you're not the same person." Finally, someone acknowledged my long hard climb to rebirth and transformation. But that rebirth is foreign to my children. They feel they are losing a mother. They are wrong. They are gaining not only a more conscious mother, but I'm forcing them to see me as a woman, a human being with frailties and pain and also love!

No longer willing to "eat my anger" or "hide my voice", I now proclaim the "I AM" that we all eventually come to. "The I AM", the essence, that IS WHO WE ARE!. Hopefully, they'll come to that day much quicker with the road map that I'm paving for them, as well as myself. If they listen. Lisa wasn't calling out of concern for me. She was calling to ease her own pain. We're all coming from ego until we learn to come from heart. An ex-husband's visit, a son's rebuff, and now a daughter coming round. Still the pain was there unable to release. "When will it release," I silently thought. I was to wait another day.

Thoughts brought me back again to the painful visit with my son. I hurriedly left his home, his back facing me. I swiftly drove away to meet Samantha. While waiting for her, I sat on a veranda at a coffee shop and watched a scene reminiscent of a poem I'd give to my recovering substance abuser clients. A woman was trying to park her car but the wheels were going into this huge gaping hole. She was unable to get out of it. The poem goes through an example of a "hole in my sidewalk." The person sees the hole, feels lost and helpless, and in a vicious cycle, not able to take responsibility for one's action, because of being unconscious. The walk down the street repeats itself, falling again and again into the same hole, but finally, one is able to see the hole, own one's faults, and subsequently walk around it and choose another street.

As with my marriage, I took another path. I finally left. I feel the entire family is better off for it. All I can say is that I have my freedom but it has come at a price. The family continues its dysfunction as if we were together. No one is quite willing to either look at the "hole" or "go around it" to forgiveness. Mother's Day came. My bird woke me up singing. I was able to hear it fully and joyously. Vita! Life! Indeed.

Life is all around me now as I write. The plant my son and his wife gave me sheds its small red roses in abundant and radiant hues. My youngest daughter's large pink azalea plant, setting in a corner on my terrace in the pickle crock I took from the house. I took it because it has the number "five" on it to remind me of the family that was. And in another corner on my terrace is my eldest's daughters plant of last year struggling to bloom in springs, and our families, mercurial weather. The heart is still paining till a phone call from my father..."My daddy..." Calling to wish me a "Happy Mother's Day." The tears begin to flow and the day is spent with brother and father.

Children are far away and on their own. "Let go, Elaine, they have their own life to lead." Sleep came easier that night.

CHAPTER SEVENTEEN:
"BODYWORK AND OLD TEARS"

Morning brought old pain, depression and weariness from sleep and dreams. I had an early appointment with my massage therapist, Tashi, whom I dearly love. No makeup on this morning. Just myself, and my body presenting to the day. Bare, vulnerable, yet strong. I eagerly awaited the table - a symbol of comfort and truth to my body, mind and soul. There is no hiding the truth to the body. It's all there, contained in skin and flesh. "Are you ready?" began the session. Very ready today! My body knew it, I consciously didn't. I discussed my painful symptoms "the shoulders, arm and left side in general." Her hands are sensors, exquisite sensors to my energy, pain, joy and sorrow. They touched my body, "Emotions. Spleen is tender." I had diarrhea Mother's Day and knew that the liver was continuing to detoxify which was confirmed by Tashi. Silence... the session had begun. Tashi worked her magic. Hands traveling up and down my spine, knowing, sensing where the pain was. Gently and firmly massaging tissue, bringing the body's suppleness alive, to the surface, to finally release in breath, exquisite breath.

Hands loosening the spine, the neck, the arms, the shoulders. I instinctively knew when to turn over, getting ready for the final half of the session. The body was now showing signs of relaxation. Work was on the front part of the body ever so more vulnerable than the back. The front of the body contains the emotions; the back - the will. The breasts, the genital area were now exposed to the world, clothed in a towel, but exposed nonetheless. Work began on the feet. Massaging the feet, was, in effect, a double massage to the body. For each organ in the body is represented in the feet, as with the ears. Now the work progressed to the wrists. My mind went to times past regarding work on them. A flick of the wrist had produced tears in the session. "None today," I thought as Tashi's hands proceeded to the Dan Tien, the "elixir of life," the lower abdomen area. It was in reworking the neck area, today more supple than usual, that produced the "old tears." A gentle twist of the neck and I was sobbing. Just as quick as that, a twist of the neck opened the floodgate. The sobs were coming from deep within. Instantly I knew these were tears from the marriage, old tears. Old tears of my son's shoulder being broken "accidentally" at four years old.

The re-connection was made as suddenly as my crying out to God early Mother's Day. Again, I was carrying and feeling pain of another. This time it was my son's pain mixed in with mine - not my mothers. I wailed, sobbed and willingly let go of the pain through the tears that furiously flowed down my face, down my neck until they were caught by quiet tissues soaking up old hurts. This continued for several minutes and then the body was calm in quiet repose.

The release was accomplished. Finally extricating the tenacious, old, rage-filled, exquisite and somehow familiar pain. I no longer wanted that familiarity. It had taken twenty-eight years to release. "Good," said Tashi, acknowledging the work we had both accomplished. "Good, indeed." Letting go of a very big piece. The pain, representing the marriage, its evilness exposed and finally evaporated out of flesh, out of blood, out of sweat of a twenty-six year old marriage. Gone! A deep sigh of relief. Finally let go of and making space in body, mind, and heart for Love, Peace, Light and Acceptance. The darkness had not and will not ever consume me; rather it will transform and transfigure me through its purging fires.

"The heart area is getting stronger," I thought, as Tashi lightly touched the breastbone. At other times the pain was excruciating in that area. There was none today. This piece of massage therapy was reflective of many things; of how the body holds "old tears," in repressed emotions, that become energy blocks. It is also indicative of the body's memory of the accident last year. The work completed, the body was at peace, as was the mind and soul. I had finally released the pain of last week's events; the body ever wise knew of the readiness for release - of the marriage, the ex-husband, the lover and the son.

CHAPTER EIGHTEEN: "BODYWORK & MOTHER"

After releasing in bodywork, I felt better. It was now May 13th. My good luck day! I again went to Tashi. "Hmn," I thought, "What's going to happen today?" Only yesterday I was racked with pains, especially in the spleen area. I'd been taking herbs and homeopathic remedies prescribed by my shaman friend, Jim, as well as Tashi. "The spleen is much better today, no soreness. It's amazing," said Tashi. The body was more supple though the original trauma in neck, arm, back on the left side is still tight. The body is responding to therapy though memories, of the accident still remain in cellular memory. That morning I had found my "Shit list" that Jim had suggested I write in order to let go of old issues via the colonoscopy. I thought I had all the items written and then put into the garbage after the procedure. But there was this one "list" left. Right on top of the list was what I had just dealt with - rage - towards my ex-husband, son, lover, as well as towards myself for the "not enoughs" in my life. Apparently, Spirit felt I needed to let it go again. I put the list on my altar and spent the day writing. That night, I began to sacredize and ritualize the list by prayer and then a burning. I read aloud my grievances, then tore them up in minute bits and pieces. Feeling that wasn't enough, I began to burn each piece thinking aloud of each hurt, burned it and flushed it down the toilet. One small piece remained. I flushed it down again. It let go. But what was the "it"? "Is it the issue with my parents? My ex-husband, son or my lover? I don't know. Perhaps, it is both my father and lover!"

Prior to ridding myself of old pains, I began to think of my book and the next chapter. I looked at all the pages I had written since my mother's vision. The manuscript's full effect suddenly penetrated every cell, memory and bone in my body. IT'S REAL! It's happening. The hoped for, intended for book is becoming reality, by being re-membered and re-cognized in my re-visiting of past issues! So that's the reason I'm reviewing old issues; to let them go and make room for life and newness through bodywork. I placed the book reverently before the statue of Mary. I silently prayed with deep knowing and feelings beyond words. I realized what day this was. May 13th. My mother. Mary. Myself. Another initiation over. My mother had come back to give me this one last sacred Mother's Day gift. My body no longer entwined in hers in a negative way. I now have my self, the book, and perhaps a sister. The promise of Mary five years ago when I asked for a miracle has been fulfilled. The prophecy realized in this last most painful process. I'm in another stage now, that of Redemption and Resurrection.

Tears of joy came to my eyes. Feelings of deep gratitude and love for my mother, myself and Mary overwhelmed me. I lay down in bed, put my "Om" tape on and slowly surrendered my body, now at peace, to sleep. "She" responded in kind as I felt a tremendous surge of energy. I can only describe it as an oceanic wave of feeling surging throughout. No longer were there any blocks. I now felt re-connected to my body. It felt wonderful.

CHAPTER NINETEEN: "MOTHER"

The early years in our three-room apartment were spent with memories of mother silently crying in her bedroom, doors closed, mouth closed, heart breaking. She never said, and I never asked, why she was crying. In hindsight how very pitiful and unnecessary that seems now. Mother and daughter prisoners in their own body afraid to ask, afraid to feel the fear. She occupied her days with housecleaning, cooking, knitting, sewing and baking. I'd remember the homemade birthday cakes with freshly sliced peaches and whipped cream for topping. Tears come to my eyes as I write this. The body knows, memories reappear, tears flow. My mother later on made magnificent dolls clothes for my daughters. And the Afghans! Everyone in our family has a memory of my mom's spirit in the Afghans she quietly presented to them.

I also have memories of our cat "Day-Day" Don't ask why the nonsensical name! He just was "Day-Day". He was only a tiny kitten when I found him wandering around the train station sub-structures down the block from our apartment. The same structures I'd climb as a youngster. My father didn't want to keep the kitten, but I prevailed. Mother, brother and I loved that cat. We would dress him up as a baby, hat, bottle, diapers and all. We would wheel him around in my doll carriage. He was quite smart. He knew when to get out of my father's way, as well as going to my mother's lap for nurturing. There was a special bond between the two of them. To see my mother with that cat was to see my mother in a totally loving light. She was especially attentive to him and he to her. The fire escape was his sole avenue for sunning himself. I especially recall one night when all were sleeping. I was awakened by a "meow" that seemed familiar but far away. The bedroom window was opened an up he went to the top floor. He was too frightened to come down. I tiptoed into my parents, and brother's sanctuary, and went up the fire escape three floors to retrieve him. Was he happy to see me! He also was quite adept at turning the hall light switch on and off. It was a switch five or so feet high near the kitchen in the hallway where my roll top desk and dresser were. How he managed this, I don't know, but he did. His other feat was that he would straddle the toilet bowl and void just like humans.

One of my closest friends, Patricia, lived in the same apartment complex on the fifth floor. I would hang out in their apartment. Her family had two bedrooms - a luxury to me. Up the stairs I'd go to her apartment for it was like a second home to me when my folks worked. Pat's mother and mine were good friends until Pat bit me through my pea jacket. They never spoke afterwards. I recall my mother at Easter time bringing me shopping for a totally new wardrobe. A new straw hat, patent leather shoes, underwear, an Easter dress, pocketbook, and, of course, white gloves! Pat and I would wonder what the weather would be like on Easter. If it rained, no new clothes. The routine was that Pat would knock on my door for our mile long walk to church. Other than Easter, I would feign sleep, not wanting to get up early and walk the long walk to church. Sometimes Pat would persist by knocking on the door saying, "I know you're in there, Cordani!" Other times she would give up. Rain enabled us to play hide and seek up and down the dual set of staircases on either side of our apartment. I particularly liked to hide on the side underneath the stairways right by the mailboxes. Again in the corner where I'd seldom be found and tagged "You're it!"

Kids would play handball in the hallways much to the frustration of the grownups. Our pastime, as well, would be outside Victor's corner grocery store. The same grocery store my mother would send me to buy food. I having to read the list many times till I'd memorize it "to heart." Next to Victor's was "the stoop," an indented two-seater portion on the side of the store. To the right of the stoop was a brick wall that we liked to play handball on. We played there till the neighbors on the first floor would throw buckets of hot water on us causing only a temporary halt. The stoop was the community center for kids in the neighborhood. We fought to sit there, and never relinquished it, except for food or sleep. "Potsie," was a pet game where one would throw a stone or some such object and jump in the boxes. I loved drawing with chalk on the sidewalks, jumping rope, especially double Dutch and roller skating. One had to have a key to tighten the skates. I still have that key. What fun!

We were raised in an Italian-Jewish neighborhood, and all got along very well. Mother had many friends. Our Jewish neighbors, and she would sit for hours knitting and teaching others how to knit. I recall with pride and fondness the argyle socks that I made for my boyfriend. The toe was bigger than the entire sock! I never knew how to cast off.

I recall going outside to play and then going past the super's home, which was down at the end of the apartment house on the corner. There was a long open alley way, then a tunnel, and out one would come to the center courtyard in the back of the house where I lived. I'd often go there to call for my mother, always making up some excuse to get the love I felt I had never received. "Mommmmmmmmy!" No answer. Again. "Mom-meeeeeeeee!" Father came. "What do you want your mother for?" I knew to ask for love in the form of a penny. The penny, carefully wrapped in newspaper, would be thrown down. Love would not. I would then go to the next corner down the block where the candy store hangout was, to buy "Love" in the form of candy. The child soon learns that food is Love. The adult now trying to unlearn and re-teach what the body knew all along. Food is necessary but love is found elsewhere.

Directly underneath our block of buildings was the boiler room, a treacherous, scary, dark place where the super would haul coal to feed the always hungry furnace. My brother used to help out there at times with the super. I bet reading this will bring back many memories for him.

It's sad to say but I don't recall my mother as a person. She was "just a mother" and always around but never there. She would clean the house, visit neighbors, or go across the street to sit in the train station promenade. The train station was grand and elegant in those days. There were hills to the left of the promenade. We'd play on them and pretend they were mountains. The promenade itself had stone seating all around the large area. In the middle was a circular stanchion, concrete seating area. I recall spending hours going round and round the flagpole feeling free and dizzy at the same time. Simple pleasures.

I especially remember the day when Pat and I and our mothers' congregated there. Pat's mother told us "don't let anyone touch you there" pointing to our genitals. We were ten or eleven at the time. "There" was the non-descriptive word for our vagina. No word anatomically, that is, would surface from our mother's lips just "down there" and "up there." Breasts and vagina were "dirty words." Breasts were something I was never proud of. I was "big for my age, up there." I was the first in my class to wear a bra, something that wasn't a source of pride for me. In fact, my arms would get tired from holding them across my "up there" area. No wonder we got the feeling that bodies and sex were dirty. What was pure? The flavor of my mother's generation was well peppered with euphemisms to describe the wonder-filled human body. I had two strikes against me at that age. I was Catholic and Italian. Shame entered the picture with such an opening.

At fifteen or so I went out for a walk with a neighbor friend of mine. My mother knew the boy. That didn't matter. In her bathrobe, over the proverbial house dress, my mother greeted me in front of the entranceway to our apartment building, and called me a whore, for no apparent reason other than it was 10pm. At that time, I didn't know about sex, much less do it! Between an Italian upbringing, my mother's silent shame, her projections onto myself at the same tender age of her secret, as well as the Catholic Church, what chance did I have of ever getting in touch with my sexuality! I had a lot of work to do in my early adult years.

CHAPTER TWENTY: "NEW HOMES"

I'm sitting on my terrace now, my bird happily chirping in his cage beside me. I am looking at the azalea plant my daughter Tracy gave me. The pink blossoms are slowly fading in spring's rush of life. I touch them gently and the flowers readily fall in my hand. They are slowly relinquishing spring blossoms to green new leaves, continuing Nature's cyclical pattern. I feel the same way about leaving my apartment finally after twelve years. This has been my "love nest," my sanctuary after the marriage. The place my lover and I could escape from pain and reality - to pain and fantasy. I loved every minute of it but "our love nest is no more," as I reverently informed him. So as with the azalea blossoms, growth needs to occur for the relationship to survive.

I recall when my family moved from our apartment to our first home. Oh, how excited we all were. My mother woke me up one night and told me that we were moving. Important events were "sprung on me" similar to my finding out about my brother's birth. There was no "process", that well worn word with much meaning, that I frequently use with patients. "We're moving." That's that! I was lying on my "branda" near the living room window in order to try and catch a rare summer breeze. I don't recall what I thought, much less felt. I was just about to graduate at sixteen years old from high school. We moved immediately afterwards.

At fourteen friends and I worked at the telephone company on Saturdays, part time for $7 a day. We would take the train that was right across the street from our apartment to Lafayette Street in New York City. We'd sit in front of a booth with many cubbyholes and sorted telephone bills. Boring as hell. When I graduated, they sent me to Comptometer School on 42nd Street. I was a wiz at those new machines. Much different than the computer I now use. "You have a thing with machines" my lover says, meaning, of course, that I was fearful. "No, I just don't like them, that's all. They're too time consuming. There's too much out in the world to see instead of being consumed by a machine that demands your constant and pernicious attention!"

I felt wonderful about moving and since I was working I bought my first bedroom set. I went to West Farms, our version of the "mall"

90

and purchased a blonde wood five piece bedroom set. At last, I had my own room and my own bed. A double bed, two night tables, a double dresser and a chest of drawers. Oh, yes, and a mirror. The chest of drawers went to my brother in his room. The rest was mine. My parents bought twin beds. They, like most other Italians in that section, were very proud of their new home. Indeed, we were ensconced in a very Italian neighborhood. Comes the summertime, everyone has a tomato garden. In fact, when we first moved there a vacant lot across the street was the community garden. It was there that we had to call the fire department to again rescue our cat, from a tall, stately tree. Those were fun times!

My first impression of the house was one of total acceptance. There were large hedges around the patch of dirt in the front yard. The house has two stories, a high pitched roof that contains an attic and a basement. The front patch of dirt now contains large bushes and seasonal flowers, a black railing and gate guarding the entranceway. There are two steps and our own "stoop" in front of the entranceway. Inside, is a glass double-door entranceway and hallway to the livingroom.

The hallway houses two stained glass windows. To the left is a picture of my mother's brother, "Willie." Willie was the most accomplished one of the five Picchioni children. At the tender age of fourteen, he was a daredevil parachutist, traveling from New Jersey to Roosevelt Field, Long Island, that now houses a huge mall, in place of the famous airstrip that once was. Willie became a senior captain at United Airlines. His career entailed highlights such as flying stunts for Charles Lindbergh in the movie "Spirit of St. Louis." Later, he was chosen to fly Lindbergh home to die in Maui. Full circle.

His accomplishments are validated by induction into the Teterboro Hall of Fame in New Jersey. I recall my mother smiling when she spoke of him taking the sisters for a spin. "It was a two-seater and your Uncle liked to do the loop-de-loop. We were so afraid," said she with a huge smile on her face. She loved it! She was as much a daredevil as her brother.

At the end of the long hallway, once one made sure to "hang up your coat" by Grandpa, one would have a last opportunity for mirror gazing into the tall hallway mirror with two Italianesque wall lamps. That was the end of any individuality once you entered the house.

91

Invariably grandchildren would find Grandma in her rocking chair by the window and Grandpa in the kitchen cooking. The smells of spaghetti gravy, fresh ravioli and Grandma's cheesecake led one straight to the kitchen after a perfunctory "Hello" to Grandma, who would invariably respond with "Yeah, yeah," which was her shy way of greeting you.

Once in the large livingroom and front parlor with its new green oriental rugs and runner by the door, one went to the left where the dining room is. The dining room is large, containing a light fruitwood French Provincial set bought from the former owners. Our old tv set now converted into a handsome credenza placed opposite the table, on the wall of the staircase that led to the three bedrooms. The staircase has thirteen very steep steps. I now think of my mother and wonder how she dragged her body up those steps each day and night.

Above the credenza hung pictures of the current Pope. This changed once my mother died. The Pope was overthrown by two of my favorite photographs my brother took which are separate photos of Mom and Dad in a sepia-print background in the kitchen, of course, preparing and/or eating food. What else in an Italian household? Mom in her favorite blue and pink new dress she ordered from a catalogue and Dad proudly serving up some dish for the holiday ritual.

Everyone knew both their seats and routine by heart. Kiss Grandma. Go in the kitchen, see what Grandpa's cooking, sneak some food before he hollers to get out of the kitchen, gobble the food down before going back to the living room, on with the TV and "plop" on the couch. Kids on the couch, adults on the chairs. Females talking to Grandma. Males of all ages looking at TV, until Grandpa came in and either announced dinner was served or brought in some appetizers such as homemade torte (spinach/rice/cheese in a thin dough). That's a favorite in our household. If one refused, you were ostracized by him. That's when Grandma would come to the children's rescue.

There's no more Grandma to do that anymore. Her picture as a smiling young woman rests in eerie silence and strong command on the radiator cover by the front window. Mom is no longer there.

The house has three bedrooms upstairs. My parents in the front room with a nice view of the Italian "commotion" outside.

Commotion is Italian's replacement for E-motion. Emotion is energy in motion and that's quite an apt description for the ruckus outside, and inside the homes and minds; my families included. It is easier to cause a commotion than to feel "paura," that ominous Italian word that struck to the core. It's easier to get sick, than to feel fear." Once I married, my father vacated his twin bed in exchange for my double bed and my room. My room was in the back of the house next to the bathroom right after you climbed the steep staircase. My room still has the same bedroom set I bought some forty-three years ago. I still visit the room to look in the mirror and get a front and back view from both the dresser mirror and the one on the door. Sometimes I like the view, sometimes I don't.

My brother's room is still the same way he left it only cleaner now. Dad used to say "I wonder what kind of doctor you are with all the mess you made in the room." My brother made a great kind of doctor. My father had a way of putting down anyone and anything other than if he liked it. Gerald's room still contains his homemade and marvelous telescope made at a young age in Stuyvesant High School, a prestigious school for gifted kids. The room also contains another "plop down fall in, falling down" bed with probably the same mattress he slept in eons ago. Nothing changes in that house only time. And there's the first tv set which contains a radio as well, ensconced in a marvelous wooden cabinet the likes of never seen in this fast food age. His bookends that I bought him are still there. No books in them now, only dusts of time.

Oh, yes, there are two other rooms. The attic upstairs which is where I found the picture of my sister in the cedar chest. The cedar chest is now down in the basement containing yet more sad memories…a wrinkled, aging, yellowed wedding dress of mine and a crystal crown headpiece similar to Princess Margaret's which was in fashion at the time. We both married in the '60's and divorced. The attic contains old things. Old furniture, old Christmas ornaments, old memories among the dust. When my mother died, I found Gerald's baby carriage clips and my small plastic doll with moveable eyes. Mother saved everything. Dad threw out everything he found. What a combination of opposites.

I suppose I need to describe the basement and the backyard as well. And the porch, can't forget the porch, my parents' window to their world. Down another steep flight of stairs is the basement, neat and sparse. There is the washer and lines to hang clothes to dry. There's the place for empty vinegar bottles to store olive oil and give to me when I leave. There's the tool room where my mother's well used cane and walker lie; aides for her daily struggle. And my father's wine cellar. In the corner of the basement lies the famous cedar chest, the cedar chest that held my sister's secret, as well as the wedding dress of mine from a failed marriage.

The kitchen has a door by my father's chair and pantry that leads to my parents', and now my father's world. It overlooks a large homemade birdbath made from a tire. You know the ones, with points on them. Every household had one then, not now, except in my parents' home. Now is then there! The birdbath sits in the midst of a modest size backyard that has grass in the middle and wherever there is dirt planted staples; Italian staples. No flowers just staples like tomatoes, string beans, lettuce that is given proudly to the family, every summer, whether you wanted it or not. That was home. It's not my home anymore. I'm moving on, and out of the Bronx. Will it ever be the same? Will I ever be the same?

I was also thinking of new homes as I traveled to see Madeline for another session of spiritual healing of my human energy field, through bodywork. I thought of the "New Homes" I had learned since the accident - that of healthier niche for my body - in the form of Yoga, Tai Chi, Qigong, herbs and acupuncture. I liked the new space afforded me in my body, especially how energetic I felt.

Madeline said that we were going to work on the hara line and my Core Star, my essence. "This will help you strengthen your sense of purpose as well as give you a firm foundation with which to withstand all the turbulent emotional issues you're currently revisiting." Well said, however, I wasn't particularly happy about that because it meant I wouldn't receive any channeling messages I so desperately wanted at this critical stage. She indicated that I'm revisiting old emotions. I spoke to her about my areas with ex-husband, lover, son, father as well as legalities regarding the accident. It's been ten months now and my pain continues but benefits are being edged out. So the work needs to be again on the self. When will it ever end?

When the session started I was thinking about food and other mundane things. Then I began to feel weird and afraid. The weirdness was in part coming from my head recalling the junk food I had in abundance yesterday. Head felt heavy. Body felt disjointed. I didn't move. Then an itchy nose. I just let it be. I then felt expansiveness, a vastness so real that I recalled the saying "Far out!" I was in the cosmos and wondered if I was ever going to return to earth. I got an image of Salvador Dali's painting with the surreal wavy clock. That's exactly how my body felt. I experienced the expansiveness as very frightening. I wanted to hold on but there wasn't anything to hold on to. My body felt as if it was floating - in all different directions. I didn't feel as if I had any skin to contain parts of me. They were scattered, floating in the universe.

In returning from this state, I understood why the move was taking so long. A "new home" not only encompasses new living quarters but requires a new and more enlightened state of being; an expanded consciousness which brings further openness, after more work!

I left Madeline with the above thoughts buzzing around my head. I needed to just rest with them. I had been searching for a new home for quite a while. Nothing comes easy or quickly, but now I knew why, for a new space has many meanings, and what is emerging is the unconscious meaning - which is stopping outward movement for now. I needed to ask myself: "What does a new home mean? What did it mean to my mother? What did it mean to my sister?" I can only answer for myself and only suppose for the others.

Afterwards, I was angry at myself for not being "enough" again. Not going fast enough, not good enough, not enough time, not enough money, not enough food, not enough support, not enough love. ENOUGH OF NOT ENOUGH! My mind tired of these thoughts! Not enough means not accepting myself and where I am. Again, it goes back to staying in the present, letting go of emotions and acceptance - acceptance of who I am and where I am - acceptance also of who people are and where they're at. Lesson learned.

What does a new home mean? It means excitement, hope and new possibilities. It means adventure. Most of all it means expansiveness. One cannot move externally without it. I had no choice in my first few moves. I was told surreptitiously that "we're moving into a house" by my mother. That was that. The next move was harder still for it meant moving with someone other than my family. It meant marriage and living with someone you know but not like family, yet. Perhaps this is why I couldn't decide whether to marry or not. In fact, I've never really addressed the marriage of twenty-six years and eleven years of single life until now. It is time to open that door, revisit and close the door with a newly found perspective. That is where I'll find acceptance and forgiveness.

I remembered my fantasy of childhood in that I was attracted to blond men. My mother never liked blonds. She said they were "weak and insecure." A projection of personal experience? We shall never know. I married a blond, good looking, intelligent, kind, caring and sexy man. The attraction was immediate. I was working at CBS, TV Business Affairs Department on Madison Avenue with all its "hype." My office was next to Ed Sullivan's which meant I got to see the stars before they went on his show which was fun.

Friends and I from there went to the Berkshires in Massachusetts for Halloween. Hoping to meet someone but afraid to the accept the possibility at the same time, I went. That evening before the social events started, we had dinner. From across the room instantaneously, in a flash of unconscious recognition, I recognized my beloved, my intended one. There he was, blond and very handsome, voraciously devouring a steak. I suddenly said to my friends "Look at that guy!" We continued dining but the image was in my memory. We dressed up as male waiters. It was easy, just a white shirt, black pants and bingo, a Halloween outfit!

I recall the very moment we first connected. Feeling quite unrestrained for some unknown reason, I saw him walking towards the barn where the dance was held. Immediately, I walked up to him, gave him a kiss on his cheek and quietly ran away. I had never done that before, and I didn't quite know what got into me. He was pleasantly stunned, smiled and went on his way. Later that evening, we again met at Happy Hour. I was tired and sat down. I had on a man's sweater and was chatting with my friends. He sat next to me and said "Are you that fat?" Usually first statements sets the tone for a relationship. I noticed he was carrying a cooler filled with beer. My first clue. We chatted a while and I left. As I did I thought how handsome he was. I questioned was this fate, destiny, choice, expansiveness? Who knows? The unconscious knows. It was there in an instant, an image or series of images, of dreams, memories, feelings, recollections of days gone by - an "imago" image of the "one" occurred.

However, he was too fast, too pushy. I gave him my number anyway especially since he only lived a few miles from me. He called. The magic words were "I'm calling from school." My ears perked up. I wanted a "white collar" worker as we said in the 50's. No "blue collar" worker for me. Again, images of past memories. We dated. We clicked. His name, Bill. He said when I opened the door of my home the first time, he knew he wanted to marry me. I didn't. For the two years we dated, he persisted in asking me each time "When are you going to marry me?" It only pressured and confused me. Lack of expansion, caution, lack of love?

I didn't know then, but certainly now, that it had to do with intimacy and leaving home. After all I was twenty years old, finally had my own room, friends and "making good money" as the euphemism goes. Why would I want to marry? The question permeated my mind. I had no yearning for marriage. I was comfortable in my nest then as I am now in my apartment. Bill was seven years older. He had visions of a family, children. Sometimes I feel that vision didn't include me, that I only was the procreator for children that he wanted. In fact, on our first Christmas he said "it wasn't Christmas without kids." I felt invalidated. Though we fought and ended the relationship many times, he'd "turn up" at places I frequented. Fate? Karma? Destiny? I suppose all of the above. After two years of dating, I finally relented.

I recall exactly where I was when I made up my mind to marry. It was at the train station with my mother one workday morning. We always traveled together–she to work as a bookkeeper at Consolidated Laundries on 96th St in Manhattan and I as Executive Secretary for CBS on 53rd St. & Madison Ave. "Mom, I won't be home tonight. Bill and I are going to Macy's on 34th St. to look at engagement rings." I don't recall how I felt or my mother's response, or her feelings; just that I was carried away by the swift and strong current of impulsivity. It had to be that way. There was no other way to move me in the marriage direction. Again, there was no external process only deep inner workings of the unconscious.

Prior to that with deep pain, confusion and questioning "What is love?," I started on my journey to find answers. First asking the local priest. His answer "Sex fades after awhile." Not much help there. My family doctor didn't even try to respond, but referred me to a Psychiatrist.

In 1959, psychiatry was unheard of especially in the Bronx. Something inside me wanted more, and so I went. It further heightened both mine, and my family's anxiety. Bill went wanting to know what was going on. I quit soon after. I recall my brother, fourteen at the time, trying to counsel me on our cellar steps, no doubt as my parents eagerly listened from the kitchen. But I had my mind made up. I was going to marry. So much for psychiatry. The psychic process was stronger than the conscious mind.

The marriage lasted twenty-six years. We have three beautiful children, Lisa, born ten months after our marriage. Andrew nineteen months after Lisa, and Tracy twenty-two months later. I felt overwhelmed and consumed. That was it. I vowed I would have as many children as God would provide. He/she was too generous. After that, I took matters into my own hands.

We went everywhere together and jointly raised them with our parents. In fact, our children had three sets of parents and were loved by all. Now there is only my father left, the rest all gone but Bill and I. Sometimes I think my kids have never known who their allegiance is to. It must have been quite confusing to them.

My biggest sadness to this day has been that "joint" custody. Good for my children, painful for me. I was young, wanting to live and "handed" them over, so to speak, to my elders, whom I had great respect for, probably more than I had for myself! When ties aren't severed from one allegiance to another this is what occurs. My allegiance should have been to my husband, not my family and so with him as well. I believed the failed marriage due to that, among other things. Our allegiance was to everyone but ourselves. We tried to please people, and the marriage and children suffered from that lack of individuation. My ex-husband was a "good provider" a prerequisite to marriage in those days; now I'm not so sure in today's economic and psychological climate. The marriage also suffered from alcohol abuse and its long tendrils through many generations. The pain drove me to therapy, school, a new career, and ultimately divorce.

My mother "handed over" her alleged child at fourteen or sixteen, if the story and psychics are correct. Strange similarities between us both. She wound up truly loving her grandchildren as she had loved her son and daughter(s)? We get another chance as grandparents to make up for the inadequacies of our unconscious ways.

What must it have been like to "hand over a child?" To know that someone else is caring for YOUR child is extraordinarily painful. I know. To have had it otherwise meant a willingness to enter and work through the shame. Not in those days; not at fourteen years old when life is beginning. Did it begin or end for my mother? And what of Grandma Rose, or Aunt Jennie, did they have a hand in the decision? Or was it the guardian of the children? I recall my mother speaking of him, can't recall his name though. And who is the father? Is he still alive? Do I have a stepfather as well? So many questions, not many answers. And what of my sister's new home? Do her adoptive parents love her? I have a very strong feeling that she never married nor had any children. Do I have nieces, nephews and an extended family? When the time is right there will be answers to this mystery.

The new home that I moved into when I married was my third move. It wasn't as drastic a move for it was only a few blocks from my parents' home. My father found the apartment for us. We had given up at that point and just wanted to go to the movies that evening. In effect, our new apartment was a gift from him. He brought oil (that life should go smoothly) and bread (that we may never be without food), and salt (that we should always have spice in our lives). The apartment had a long, narrow kitchen, a large livingroom off the entranceway, and to the right of the livingroom was a tiny room where our first child, Lisa, slept. Off the livingroom was a bathroom and bedroom. We had a kitchen and bedroom set, but no livingroom furniture. It didn't matter, we were in love. We enjoyed our new home and our new love. We fought a great deal but we had love to mend it. Our marriage was a passionate marriage, at times too much so.

Lisa was born on August 17, 1961, the day the Berlin Wall was erected. The nurse handed me this tiny baby and said "Remember, your husband came first." I tried as best I could to remember. Sometimes it was easy; other times hard. The first ten years of marriage were good. After Andrew was born on March 22, 1963 we began looking for a new home. Andrew had just had his first birthday in our apartment in the Bronx, when we found our home. I didn't want to leave my parents, but my husband prevailed. It was the right decision And Tracy was conceived soon after we moved. She was born on January 9, 1965, another Capricorn like her mother. We'd kid and say she was the "Virgin Birth," because I felt it couldn't be possible that I was pregnant again! It came as quite a shock. However, I recalled an Italian folklore that said when one experiences a new move, usually one becomes pregnant. I conceived Tracy practically the first night in our home. Now I was going to have three children, just like my mother.

Our house, a brand new home, was in Rockland County which seemed so far away. The house was a colonial, yellow and white trim, with black shutters, three bedrooms, living room, diningroom, kitchen, basement and a large parcel of land...for our children to play in. We moved into the house on April Fool's Day, 1964. Most of the marriage was spent in an unconscious state. The shock of being married, having three children close to one another, left me in a daze. I became the ultimate homemaker trying to emulate my mother, and other Italian Goddesses or to please the Goddess, with a clean home, or a guilty conscience. Perfect home, perfect kids, perfect marriage. Everything had to be perfect so as not to look at the shadow side of things.

The children were treated well. Though I tried, I felt as if my affectionate ways were rejected. Emotions were something that I could speak about but not show them. I was dismissed for being "too emotional" which they got from their father. They had the best of clothes, money no object, and lots of vacations. We raised our children with loving European grandparents. There was grounding from both sides. My husband with his multi-ethnic background of German, Swedish, Finnish, Irish and English, and I with 99% "pure" Italian origin, the rest being French from my maternal grandmother.

Creativity and hobbies were spent either at home sewing, wallpapering, baking, gardening, or spending money. Our home was beautiful especially when we added a huge comfortable family room off the dining/living room. We had a fireplace, slate floors and "love seats" in front of the fireplace. To the back of the family room was an area reserved for parties and tables as well as my sewing machine. And, of course, the Christmas tree every season. Andrew would have his trains around the tree. I still recall the ice skater statue I brought from my parent's home. It's still in the house I left. I need to retrieve that one day.

The magnificence of today, Memorial Day, brings me to the crest of Hook Mountain. The stone cliffs form a jagged edged sculpture. In front of this awesome sight are purple large trees in full bloom. The din of people are down at the base of the river. It's quiet up here on this sunny day. Reminiscing about my marriage leaves me sad and flat. Emotions will surface in dreams, food and sleeplessness tonight. What's done is done. Integrate the good, let go of the rest, accept and forgive, Elaine. There is goodness in each one of our family members and similar to the "commotion" of Italians in the Bronx, "e-motion" is played out in "acting out" behavior. There's no talking of the pain everyone feels about the marriage. Similarly, there is no acceptance or forgiveness. But Love will ultimately prevail. It always does.

A plane suddenly appears, magnificently diving, and then suddenly soars above and beyond the jagged cliffs, flying free, as if reaching to the Heavens. This much I wish for all of us, and may our minds have new homes as well on our new and separate paths.

CHAPTER TWENTY-ONE: "LEAVING HOME"

Leaving my home was easy once I made the decision. However, the decision took more years than it took to marry. I didn't want to disrupt my children's childhood. Also, how could I leave when Catholics don't divorce, especially Italian Catholics. Of course, and thank God, security never entered into it. Security never was an option in any of my decisions. I always led with the heart. Leaving the marriage was the same way. I would threaten to leave, but never did. Instead, leavings were either going to college or away on weekends by myself, or losing myself in binging so I wouldn't feel the pain.

I never actually could summon the courage of my firm conviction that leaving would be the best for everyone. That is, till I met my lover. I met him and soon after I made the decision to leave. He was my catalyst but wasn't the sole reason for leaving. The decision really had nothing to do with him. What he afforded me was a window of seeing the world through different eyes. He still does. I respected my husband, and myself too much to be either adulterous nor hypocritical. I would not do that to him, the family, my lover and myself. In fact, my lover was quite objective enough to discuss the leaving, saying he didn't want me to leave because of him. I love him for being that way. I shall always love him. He brought out the woman in me. Through him I learned to both love myself as well as him, as unconditionally as I ever loved anyone. As he used to say "You have that effect on me." And he too on me.

The actual leaving came in a flash. I had gone to an art exhibit with friends at my former college. The day flowed. I had a wonderful and freeing time - the expansiveness I had been afraid of now felt right. The decision had now solidified in my mind. I returned home to give my husband the news. He, at first, didn't believe me. However, that same day he went to a realtor as I did a half hour later. You can imagine my amazement when I saw his car in the realtor's driveway as I pulled up. Needless to say, the sales people were uncomfortable. It was both funny and surreal at the same time. However, it felt right.

We sat in the office and discussed the same apartments we both separately saw. That was the beginning of exhibiting healthier relations between us than we had ever done in our marriage. It has enabled us to be at our children's events in a much more adult, and comfortable way. It was a testimony to our deep love for one another, a love that survived the turmoil of the marriage but one that precluded us ever living together into the old age both had dreamt about, never worked towards and subsequently never shared. My values and beliefs subtly changed as I went out into the world.

I chose to leave though I was a student and not earning a living yet. I chose to leave to end a chapter and afford myself an opportunity for a new beginning. I also chose to leave for I didn't want to fight anymore. I wanted to live and live peacefully. I chose to leave because I had a life. My husband's life was wrapped up in the life we had had when our children were small. The leaving was not felt till much later.

That last night at home my husband came into my bedroom and on his knees appealed to me not to leave. I vividly recall that moment. I had to be strong. It was the right decision but very painful, painful to this day.

A different pain had now begun, once the shock wore off. The abyss I had spoken about was now in full swing; one that would mirror now only my behavior not others. One day in summer school while sitting in class, the full extent of my actions took hold; a hold that while deepening made me aware that there was light at the other end. I hung on.

And so I left. Left to go to a new life, a beautiful apartment, continue my schooling for another year and help support myself by housecleaning, something I knew very well. My children were grown and all out of the house but Tracy. My life was hard but better. There was peace in my new home, a peace I long fought for in my marriage but it never prevailed. I needed to let go and move on to find peace for myself, no longer a family unit, shorn of my status as a "Mrs," shorn of financial abundance but gaining myself in the wrenching free of a failed marriage. Hardly a word can describe the pain in the heart and soul, for I had made a vow when I married to Mary. On my wedding day I presented Her a bouquet of flowers that this was to be forever. Forever came too soon. Forgive me, Bill. Forgive me children. I did the best I could.

CHAPTER TWENTY-TWO: "LOVE'S TEST"

I'm staring at a water pitcher my mother brought back from my parents' trip to Italy in 1964. I use it each day to water my plants but I never really took notice of it. Italy is an unknown to me even though I'm Italian. My roots are well grounded in family ties, especially emotions, but not much in heritage until now for emotions get the best of me. I have my mother's letters from the trip. I have her "book" as well which is a chronological detailed account of dates of births, deaths, weddings, anniversaries, etc., of my parents' family. I know what it says but I haven't really "digested" it yet. For one thing, there are few sentences with emotion in them - like my Grandmother "was a good apple pie baker" and her father "would take the family out." That's it.

An incredible sadness of her life overwhelms me. Was there any happiness for her after all her early losses? I know she was close to her sister and brothers for we would routinely visit New Jersey, the same state my alleged sister lives in.

As for myself, once I left my house, not my home anymore, I went into deep soul searching. My life was totally changed. I had a year left of Graduate School for Social Work, settled into my "nest" quite rapidly and worked part-time housecleaning. Studies took up a major part of my time. And there was time, as well, for my lover. He's never met my family or friends. It's been our "cocoon" relationship for many reasons. He's always lived with another woman and dated (no, that's too strong a word), "seen" me all the while his numerous liaisons were occurring. I had no idea what I was getting into until I was "hooked." I still am. All I knew was from the first moment I set eyes on him, he affected me. At first, negatively. We had occasion to work together and I found him cynical, arrogant and pompous and told him so. I also found him quite handsome and I was charged with electricity each time I saw him. In fact, after I spoke to him I sped down the parkway at 80mph with radio blaring and windows open. Yes, I was "hooked", though I knew nothing about him. It didn't matter. It still doesn't.

The first time we met he had an Afro and a cigarette holder. He was nothing I would have been attracted to had I the choice, but I hadn't. He came to me. It was, I believe, providential. I had called him into my life. I never regretted that calling. It is a testimony of my love for him, a love that is both mysterious and unrequited. It has the same flavor as the yearnings I had for Bill when we'd break up prior to our marriage. I suspect it has to do with my early images, whether parental or otherwise, of my own lack of fulfillment.

He sat next to me one day and pursued me to a point, handing me his business card. "Who is this man?," I thought. What arrogance! A real salesman. He pursued me to a point, that is. The next step was all mine. I went forward with a great deal of focused awareness, knowing full well that it would change me. I went through the fear.

I was working on research regarding weight recidivism, a final project of mine before graduating. Research was a new way of looking at things, and one that baffled and scrambled my mind. So much so, that I took him up on his offer to help me. Help he did. He met me and I knew before the meeting that I was in trouble. I had called him from home. I was at my kitchen window. While he heard my voice, I heard his hesitation. "But you promised to help me." He took a long pause, and a deep drag on his cigarette and said, "And where shall we meet?" That stopped me dead in my tracks. Though it was to be, or so I thought, a friendly meeting, the clandestine aspect froze me. I fumbled, he took up the slack. "Shall we meet in your office." Good thinking. I phoned my friend, and spoke to my therapist, but neither stopped me from going forward. My mind was made up. However, I was very clear in that "I was entering an abyss," which is what I told friends. I had been living apart from my husband for years, but under the same roof. I met this man who was later to become my lover, and left my husband soon after.

It was a Friday afternoon, 5pm. Most people had left for the day. I was quite anxious. A car door slammed outside, and footsteps were entering the three stairs in the hall down from my office. He was whistling. "How can he be so calm," I thought, while I was perspiring profusely all over my body. He strolled into my office. My supervisor was nearby in her office. I wished she would leave so we could have the place to ourselves and I wouldn't feel so guilty. But she didn't. I felt like a young school girl not the forty-seven year old married woman, mother of three children, and graduate school student. I had on my corporate look that the secretary would laugh at, saying "You don't look like a social worker. They wore long dresses,

105

dangling earrings and sandals." I suppose I wasn't ever going to fit any image. That was my challenge; to be me despite what role I was in.

I met him half way down the hall and shyly made small talk. As usual, his charming self, his gangly but graceful walk melted my heart as he comfortably seated himself at my desk, took off his sandals, put on his glasses, and said he would "be out to lunch, so to speak reading my research report." That was what I needed. Someone to take me seriously and be interested in what I had to say. He read my work and made genuinely interested and helpful comments.

I was trembling with fear as well as excitement. I took him out to dinner. I was so nervous, that I lost my shoe while heading to my car. As we were walking to our respective cars, he said he had been adopted and that he was very sensitive and hid it behind a callous exterior. He was preparing me for what was later to be our challenge.

I had the ability to see beyond the outer, though the outer had a certain appeal as well. When he put his hand on my arm at dinner, I felt that I had flown straight to the heavens. His touch went to my very core. At dinner he spoke of his marital circumstance and asked to see me. I replied in the negative, reiterated that I was a married woman, and an affair was not what I either wanted or could do. It went against both my beliefs as well as my upbringing.

But love overruled that. Inevitably I chose a new road, one through much fear, but filled with blind fate. It has gone through many tests and survived many years, but now the butterfly wants to fly free from our cocoon - with him alongside me. That has yet to happen, if ever.

What has emerged is a genuine caring and sharing of the time we have together. I came into my womanhood with him. He has yet to figure out what I mean to him. I have learned to express my anger with him, and let it go quite easily. I have learned to stay in the present for whenever I tried to shake up things, it always backfired. I have learned to let go of controls with him. I continually ask my Higher Power for help. Of course, I continually try at the same time to take back the controls until yearnings produce patience, acceptance and wisdom.

Leavings were a part of our pattern. Two years ago I told him I was moving on, sensing another leap into the unknown to produce change in my life. "Is that an ultimatum?," said he. No, I was just stating my position and that I couldn't continue seeing him. The pain was too great and we parted. He was ever with me in sight, sound, smell, touch and especially songs. All of them were like emotion filled containers that filled up and spewed over with heartfelt pain and an aching to see him.

The sameness had been comfortable to him, but I wanted more. In the ensuing power struggle we parted. In his usual manner, he'd just get up and leave my apartment. This time, not being able to bear another leaving, as with my mother's sudden death, my anger propelled me to leave him. In a way it was an empty but symbolic leaving. No one triumphed and we both missed one another. Six months went by. He pursued, I relented. We then began again.

I recalled once when we had endured a year apart from one another. Until one day while putting the key in my mailbox, I suddenly had a sense I'd see him that night. I pushed it away, not wanting to get hurt again. That night at 10pm he called asking if he could stay the night. I was delighted. However, we both couldn't sleep. I wonder, could we ever live together?

This time I called him. I had my colonoscopy, letting go of my issues and eagerly awaiting new life. Feeling relieved and relaxed, I happily went to him. Time was correct for he was thinking of me just the day before. For now, we're just happy to be together. But I've changed. I accept it for what it is much more than ever before. I have mastered my ambivalence towards him. Finally! I'm still in love with him. I cherish and adore him.

I always will. I'm fond of telling him that "I'm practicing on you... for a real relationship." Inside, I wished HE would be the "real relationship!" However, for now, it still remains a mystery. A mystery that can't wait!

At a time when I could no longer bear all the unknowns in my life, I finally relented and consulted a psychic. I was told my lover is not willing to risk; the same risking that I have taken. He has to learn and speak his truth. I am to meet someone new "nerdy" and "coming from a rock. There is no need to look for him, he will find me.

I have met someone new, very nice, caring and quite spiritually evolved who is "nerdy" and indeed "came from a rock." Nothing has come of it. Probably because I still cling to my lover but at the same time I am open to newness. I'm still in love with my lover; however I can't make him love me. Love has to be given freely. The passion is still there. Cocoons do that. But cocoons stifle reality.

To me, "reality is the best fantasy of all." I found that in a magazine article that reminded me of him. In it, there was a tall man with his back to the camera. He was bathing his small child. The tenderness of the photograph emulates the tenderness I have for him. No matter what he does, love is never shaken. It's confounding to me. My ex-husband could do no right; my lover no wrong. I wish I could see more good in my ex-husband but I can't. Perhaps the difference is that I never felt accepted as a person by him. My lover accepts me whether fat, skinny, happy, sad or in-between. He accepts me for who I am, which is important to me. I need that. Through him, I've learned unconditional love and acceptance; both for him and myself. Time will tell where the relationship will go. As much as I have a sense of things, this relationship has both of us mystified. For now, that is. I am free to come and go as I please. I don't know if he can do the same.

CHAPTER TWENTY-THREE:
"PONDERING THE MEANING OF THINGS"

Diaries and autobiographies have great meaning to me and are my usual tools for pondering my life's journey. During my marriage, a diary was started to contain my painful and confused life. Later, once I left my marriage, I started a semi autobiographical novel with two female characters, in the mental health field. One was myself as an innocent young Social worker, the other a whole and integrated mature woman. I encountered writer's block and stopped the novel. However, the diary continued, now more seriously since my separation and divorce from my husband. I needed an outlet of expression, especially working in mental health with its barren wasteland of forgotten people in forgotten bodies with forgotten minds, hearts and souls which was certainly a perfect place to plant seeds.

I felt as if I had reached my goal of becoming a therapist, and then took a step back after that goal was reached. I felt lost. There weren't any new goals, only hard work, lack of energy and a continuing depression which is where my passion had actually lodged. I was in the birth canal; the empty, dark, foreboding unknown so like that of creative new beginnings. However, I didn't know it at the time. A necessary time of waiting, going within to retrieve lost or unexpressed parts of oneself had begun.

I went into survival mode. Indeed, I was fond of saying: "Back to basics, food, clothing, shelter." I was forty-seven years old and certainly not looking forward to fifty at all! No longer the female, Italian Catholic "good girl with the rosary beads and white gloves." No longer feeling disoriented or disintegrated, but still feeling very much at sea with life in general. On the other hand, what I wrote in my diary and my naive attempt at a first book came to the forefront; the young woman suddenly awakens one day to feel that events changed the character of reality. A veil had been lifted from my eyes. Internal work had turned another page in my life's story. I had many feelings, first energized, thinking of where I'd been and how I had come to the place I could finally call my own, as well as a sense of uncertainty for the future. What I found in all of this was one could not rush this profound process, no matter how much I tried. Both psychological, as well as physical birth would come later.

However, as I look back I had my psychological birth several times. The most significant were in leavings. Leaving home, marrying, leaving my marriage, beginning school, starting a new career, and opening up my private practice. Indeed, it's the pregnancies that are painful, not the births. What I didn't realize was that I was revisiting my adolescence at forty-seven! And thus the reason for my lover's appearance.

Now that the tumultuous years of my marriage were behind me, I had time to concentrate on my career. In the beginning, I was filled with eagerness similar to the young character in my book. The experiences in social work took up the space left in my heart from the marriage. I loved my patients and they me. I took to working with all patients with an openness and creative style. At times this "style" got me in trouble with my supervisors. After all, I was at least their age or older. I soon found out that an older woman is a threat.

I worked with the developmentally disabled. They taught me simplicity and appreciation of small things in life. That was my first year of study. The next year brought me to a psychiatric in-patient unit. I learned about families from a position of distance from my own family. It stirred up feelings around my issues, both individual and familial. I began to understand each person's role in both my family as well as the ones I worked with. I learned through the pain and grew. I poured my heart and soul into everything I did. Without looking for it, it was returned to me a hundred-fold.

There wasn't a patient I didn't like, much to the disbelief of my supervisor. There were patients of all ages. On my first day on the psychiatric unit, my patient, an elderly woman with my mother's name tried to commit suicide by swallowing wooden dominoes. That was quite an initiation. I soon learned about sadness, ageism and loss. There were psychiatric youngsters that had difficulties moving on in life whether in high school or college, and many substance abusers with hearts of gold yearning to be loved but afraid to risk and reach out. And the father who attempted to murder his developmentally disabled son. He had traits similar to my husbands and I began to understand both father, son, and my ex. The son, all six feet, five inches of him, was "huffing and puffing", quite angry and threatening in our initial interview. I had some quick thinking on my side to use a ploy to leave the room. I asked him if he wanted a cigarette? When he said "Yes," thankfully, I ran down the hall to get help. He apologized for his anger, and afterwards, we worked well together.

The family I treated had a happy ending, as mine sadly had not... Family meetings were very successful. I liked to see families come together. Father now accepted and understood his son. And the young man was one of the few people who "graduated" from his group home placement and found a job. He would return to visit me on the unit where we met, quite proud of his achievements, as was his father. My pain was beginning to both help others and heal my heart and soul as well, though I didn't know it at the time. I was so engrossed in treating people that I couldn't feel my own sadness. It resided in the deep cellular recesses of my body.

There was the young girl whom I asked on her first day on the unit to keep a journal. The very next day she came back and told me she had been raped by her father, as well as having several abortions. She would heal from her trauma after an extended stay on the unit. And the father of a developmentally disabled girl who was in angst about the decision to place his daughter in a group home after being institutionalized for twenty years. He died soon after having happily made the decision, after seeing her thrive in her new environment. The AIDS patient who tried to kill herself two times in one day; first with a scalpel and then by drinking liquid bleach. And the only patient that our team treated that committed suicide...by jumping out of a tenth floor window. The staff grieved this loss and took it quite personally wondering if there was anything else we could have done. But there were some we just couldn't save.

Oh, the pain in my body from it! My neck ached and my body was sending out signals that I couldn't ignore. Where was I going? What was I to do? I now felt stuck in a web of frustration and paralysis. The paralysis was total. My body and therapy was rigid. I needed to actualize but didn't know quite how to do it. The time was coming when the good little child wanted to take steps towards womanhood and claim her wholeness. The time for birth was near and it was to come in a very unexpected place - the body!

After my lover left one night, a strange event occurred while I lay in bed for my back had been hurting. I had been sleeping in a fetal position.   Suddenly, there erupted a sound from my vagina that reminded me of a human voice. It was an actual "popping" sound. My body was opening up, calling me onward to more challenging experiences. The inner longings were so powerful that they were waking up the body. I was no longer in control; my body was.

The child of yesterday was once again being awakened. The child was crying out for re-discovery, re-birth and re-creation. This is what adults so long for.   It's the innocence of those open and joyful freedom years that have long since faded in adults' minds. The play years are gone, not easily retrieved unless one is vigilant.   The external play may be there but its adult play. What one yearns for is the internal play that goes on in the child. The ability to be creative, to make light of something, to laugh.

My inner child was experiencing openings in other areas. For my body knew before the conscious mind that it was now time to move on.   One experience on the psych unit highlights my yearnings. A young schizophrenic patient was about to be discharged. He was very gentle, loving and caring. While conducting the morning community meeting, I heard a bird chirping outside the iron bars of the unit. I thought how free that bird is! What a lovely vision - a bird's singing outside the "gates of the mind" eliminating barriers - of bars, of minds, of souls - all equal in the softness of the heart! My passion was transferred to the youngster who was leaving…to "always remember the bird when you feel sad. You're now free to do what you want. Don't let them put the bird in a cage again. The bird needs to be free, to fly, to experience, to explore, to create. You are that bird." I recall his face when he got on the elevator. It looked timid and fearful but I had a sense he was hopeful as well.

I hadn't yet realized I yearned for that freedom as well! After all, first I was the parentified child, then the parent, and at times dual parents, to my children, and now to my patients. I had freedom and longing issues but they surfaced in the form of depression and unknown yearnings. The longing for something once experienced and now gone. These are the longings of yesterday, of the lost child, and the core self.   The creativity and passion had again to be retrieved, not only for my patients, but for myself. However, I didn't have time to think of myself during those years.

Hope waned while working on the psych unit. I needed to move on. A position in the Alcohol Out-Patient Unit prompted my social work chief to suggest I apply. "I'm backing into the job," I told the director of the unit in the interview. She had a puzzled and somewhat comical look on her face when she asked me what that meant. I responded "Usually the alcohol staffs behavior parallels the dysfunction of the patients." Her head bobbed, nodding in agreement.

There was unfinished business on that unit, as with my parents in my returning to the Bronx. But after three years, and a serious fall at work, my body again was urging me to move on...this time by physical pain and fearing that my body as well as my soul would be killed off if I remained. The parallel process that I spoke of was also in the mental health system. Unknowingly, probably with good intentions, patients were culled as shadow bearers of the world's pain...and not only patients, but staff as well, for values once cherished and long since discarded; such as sensitivity, creativity and mysticism.

My job on the unit was threefold; treating individuals and groups, day treatment patients, and triage, which meant interviewing people who came in off the street to determine placement. It was a rigorous, demanding and yet a very gratifying job. As I had voiced in my interview it was a different story with the staff,. Days were spent fighting with staff about "policy" which meant whatever the people in control wanted at the time - and the line workers would have to fend for survival needs, similar to a Post Traumatic Stress Disorder situation. There was apathy, rage, and frustration, mine, as well as others!

This wasn't what I wanted with regard to treating people. Treatment became a challenge, one tried to work out on a minute-by-minute basis. Where would I go? How would I get out and support myself at the age of fifty-five? I was stuck and knew it. I didn't want to fight, for to fight meant that I had to address my rage. What was my rage about? The years had passed and I had followed my dream to become a therapist. But the dream had quickly turned to a nightmare with political maneuvers. All I wanted was to be with my patients and help them heal. I now was beginning to feel tired, old and especially, discarded. Age was possessing my soul with its symptoms of weariness permeating my very bones.

My passion for writing seemed also to have faded. There was a time when I would sit at my desk and anger and passion would meld with pen and paper in a cathartic and creative experience. That didn't seem to be the case anymore. I questioned where my passion went. It went to my patients. Indeed, I had none left for myself! Negativity was beginning to creep in as well. I needed new goal; goals to look forward to, to hope for, someone to care for. I was waiting for someone to rescue me. I needed to rescue myself. The start of my new world, a strange, frustrating world would begin several years hence. Since my return from the Cape, a vacation that was a turning point in my life, the energy gained there would soon manifest itself into the need to change, to let go, to empty out for yet more of infinite and new beginnings.

New beginnings for me are born from a long, dreamlike, fearful, and almost frozen confused state of being. Retreating to a place of nurturing was what I needed to get out of my "slump." Perhaps a more positive word for "slump" would be "slumber," the period of dreamland in which incubatory processes give way to creativity. My yearnings were to continue the momentum that had begun after the Dream Seminar. In the past, I'd retreat to the Cape. However, this beckoning was different. I heeded it in another way; a way that would present itself in a most unusual form.

I was embarking on a new chapter in my life, to a different facet of consciousness that of a transpersonal nature, which meant a partnership with ego and Spirit. My life was to enter the realm of shamanism, heightened with a future meeting with Jim at Kripalu. I didn't know that at the time. What I did know was that I felt a deepening sense of awe and definition of the process.

For the past six years friends on my former unit in psychiatry were tired of hearing me say that I was leaving. But once the decision was made, all the pieces fell into place. Leaving both parents and my job were initial catalysts, followed by the Universe and Elide with a part-time job after I left the Alcohol Unit.

The time had come. My psychological work with parents and the substance abuse unit was complete. I told no one at work where I was going. They didn't deserve to know. All I said was "suffice is to say I'm going to a job with half the hours and twice the salary!" The ending process was quite interesting. Though most people on the unit weren't supportive, several colleagues asked for my office, as well as some of my furniture. They wanted what I had, only they didn't know it wasn't material, it was spiritual! I gave it willingly, knowing full well they could have my memories, however, they could not have my soul, spirit, body or energy anymore. I would not be drained of that. I fled the job, feeling life once again as I did.

New beginnings provided open doorways. Each action promulgating new opportunities. The shamanic journey unknowingly begun while I was married now continued. It moved along a parallel course in finding hope that my mother had lost, to love; a love that I was now prepared to give to self. For when the marriage was in full painful bloom, the bloodstain that suddenly appeared AND QUICKLY DISAPPEARED on my white blouse proclaimed the need to give to myself. My initial reaction was for the safety of my children. The deeper meaning was to seek self love.

Seeking meanings led me again to question love. My path, ironically, again led me to a Catholic priest. His response wasn't helpful for he said I should lose weight and that eventually if I didn't resolve the marriage issue, I'd lose my children. I also was led to Corinthians 13, from my daughter's friend's mother, which bespeaks of love. However, my fear and confusion didn't allow love to enter my very being. At that time, I was taking a course in Spirituality, and the professor suggested it was a stigmata. I recall my classmates reaction, that of a deafening silence. That only further confused me and left me feeling like an outsider. Whatever the suggestions, I continued my journey of love and hope.

Many years later, I did leave my marriage. This time directing the questioning to God, as well as my own values and beliefs. They led to giving a workshop entitled "What Is Love?" A man and three women came. The man questioning sex, the women spirituality. Both on the same track - just different portals to the same discovery...God is Love.

The query "What Is Love?" that began in my 20's before marriage, now further intensified in my 40's and 50's. In order to find the answer, I found out "What Love Isn't!" The marriage proved that. My search continued. I volunteered in a nursing home. It was there that I began to find answers.

Peter and Michael, brothers aged ninety-five, and ninety years young, at the time, were to me the epitome of love. They selflessly gave of themselves. I spent six wonderful years there while attending college full-time for Gerontology. Their unending love supported me through the stormy marriage. When Michael died at a hundred and three years of age, Peter said "So soon!" Five days later he joined his brother. Before doing so, at the time of Michael's burial, a sudden wind forcefully entered the room and exited through the window. The young boy sweeping the floor turned ghostly white. Words came out of my mouth but not from me..."Don't be afraid, that's Michael's spirit saying goodbye."

It was eerie but somehow understandable. Peter kept looking at a blank wall and when I asked what he was looking at he said "The Light." He and Michael met death as they had life; straight on, with little fear, much courage and hope.

Once that chapter ended, another opened with meeting my lover. Another step in Love's journey was to begin, for he would be the vehicle with which we both found the Holy Grail; for suddenly my passion ignited with an overwhelming flame of desire that propelled me out of the marriage and into his arms. My journey to selfhood had begun.

CHAPTER TWENTY-FOUR:
"TURNING POINT TO NEW BEGINNINGS"

My new position in an Out-Patient Mental Health Clinic was a dream come true. The clinicians were professional, supportive, and very funny! The patients were super. The female Director of the Unit was very supportive of her staff, unlike the place I just left. What a great move I carved out for myself. I was working part-time, getting extensive experience in psychotherapy both with individuals and groups. But during one team meeting, valiantly gasping for breath, the Director suggested I needed to see a doctor. After many years I finally put a name to the "sounds in the night" that had plagued me. It was asthma. I immediately gave up cigarettes without looking back. It was at that point that I began to take more of an interest in my body.

The temp job at the clinic extended for another four months was coming to an end. And with it, I consciously experienced first-hand the power of projection. I hadn't a job and the staff was concerned for me. I wasn't, for I knew I wanted a private practice. I hadn't intended this opening, which was another of the Universe's gifts. I was getting used to endings at this point. In fact, I liked them for I never knew what would happen next! In addition, my clients could come with me. And so, I had a ready-made practice effortlessly given to me once I let go. I also knew I wanted an office by the river and at the last minute I got one!

My private practice began. It was a dream come true. I had worked towards this goal since entering Social Work School. I was no longer fearful but proud of my recent accomplishments. Finally, a practice where I'd be free of all restrictions. It was the opening to a new world, an effortless world that comes with letting go and one that I had long yearned for. My professional career was now in MY hands. A further step along the road to autonomy. But when I opened the door to my office on the first day and looked at the river, I said "There's something else." That strange statement remained with me for three years until my accident. I hadn't traveled the transpersonal journey alone. I was now quite consciously aware of God's presence in my life.

At the same time, my youngest daughter's engagement and wedding were the unmasking of many unpleasant memories and events. The weight began to creep on. Thirty-five pounds that I had lost was now reappearing. My fears precluded any sense of controls. My daughter's marriage induced many unresolved issues about my own marriage. The ghosts of the past were rearing their heads. Her leavings conveyed remnants of my adolescence never consciously evoked, but now was presently living. I helped Tracy resolve inner conflicts outwardly symbolized by which type of headpiece she would wear. I knew her choice of a crown was a symbolic statement of her transition from a young single girl to budding womanhood. It was unfortunate that "crowning" unconscious issues of both of us, caused her fury toward me for wearing a hat to her wedding. Our individual headpieces had caused conflict instead of celebration. Instead of joy, there was competition. My daughter felt I was trying to upstage her which wasn't the case at all. I looked the best I had in years and hats are a part of who I am! In fact, I used to wear them to church when the children were younger. So much for happy events, that always turn sour.

My beloved daughter ignored me the entire day. Food now contained the pain. But there wasn't any healing. Just further pain. I cried the entire five hour trip home. I had so many disappointments. Two years hence, my son wouldn't dance with me at his wedding, saying he didn't know what I would do on the dance floor! And two weeks later, my eldest moved to Louisiana.

My head was spinning. My heart aching. It was the beginning of my disconnection from my children The events around the wedding, my weight gain and bodywork were internally working for further growth. The focus was now on my body and emotions connected to the weight gain. It was my fifty-sixth birthday. I gave myself a birthday present of attending a workshop. The presenters were Myron and Joan Borysenko, who have a scientific and psychological background. They're pioneers in the newly emerging body/soul paradigm, called psychoneuroimmunology, a long word denoting the body and soul connection with the immune system. They spoke to that topic, especially about the immune system and emotions. That deepened my interest.

I recall going to the bookshop during intermission to buy some books on somatic healing. When I came back to join the group, there was a Singing Bowl, a Tibetan sounding instrument that the

Borysenko's used in the morning's meditation. It being strung by a wooden mallet around the rim's circumference by a member of the audience. I immediately clutched my heart. I was informed that my heart chakra was being purified. What better way to begin than by opening up my heart. It certainly needed an opening but one that would protect me as well during the healing process. Later, in an experiential exercise, I connected with a healer with the same name as mine. The message became clearer. Look within to the body for answers. She was starting a practice in energy work, and invited me to come. I ran there.

And so the adventure into this "thing below my neck" began. It has resolved many issues especially with my mother and provided me with experiences and symbology with which to further understand self and the world. It was there that I had the first rebirthing experience, and discovered the power of imagery.

The events around the wedding, my weight gain and bodywork were now connecting for new growth in a very different, and challenging area, that of my body! The focus was now on emotions which were suffused in the body. It was time to let these feelings emerge, in an area I had diligently protected with overeating. My soul, as well as my body, were fighting in a territory I didn't want to enter. The battle had begun!

CHAPTER TWENTY-FIVE:
"HALF-PACKED AND READY TO GO!"

March brought me to Madeline's again. I had received an increase in my rent which was the impetus I was waiting for. It was telling me that the time had come to move. That, along with the unbearable construction noise from the Thruway during early morning hours, were the catalysts. I asked Madeline to channel for any information on my future surroundings. She saw a small house with concrete, bricks and tar, a field to the right down a slope, and the number nine. And so, I went searching for my new home looking for the signs she had received. I began a tour of both Rockland and Orange County; maybe, I thought, to live near my son. I toured the coastline of Jersey where Elide lived. I found a new place in the northern section of Rockland that excited me, called Tompkins Cove. I looked at places in Piermont, and house sharing in Nyack. None was to my liking. It was as if I were redesigning my needs and wants and what I was deserving of. Nothing came of it.

During late winter and early spring, I'd go to Hook Mountain for solace and meditation. There were times I began to beat my chest as in Tarzan and Jane movies! This wasn't like me, I thought! What is happening? Whatever it was, it felt right. Actually, I got a kick out of it. What was occurring was re-connecting with my animalistic, primitive nature and primitive emotions that were later to surface. It felt quite freeing. I picked up magnificent wooden sticks carved by nature with wind and water which I put on my car's dashboard. At some point, while at a car wash, a Haitian man saw my two treasured creations, and asked for one. I believe he felt it was magical. I quickly gave him one and that was my magic!

While at the Hook one day, I spotted a huge piece of driftwood and picked it up. It was my symbolic staff of life. When I saw Madeline she confirmed that message without my telling her about it. So I was staking a claim, and the healthy part of me knew it. The other part was OK with it too. I wasn't threatened yet!

I wanted to let go of almost everything material. I held an apartment sale. I sold clothes, jewelry, shoes and other items. It felt quite freeing. I attempted to sell my bedroom set but there weren't any takers. Perhaps I needed to hold onto the remnant of my former marriage for a time. The inward harvesting of aged and ripened planted seeds, were now externally manifesting. I kept on packing, feeling "filled to the brim" with "things." I gave away and cleared still more items. Nothing came in my search for a new home. I tried to be more active. I went to several realtors in the county. I was shown many a lovely home. Ironically, the search began to narrow down to my hometown, Nyack. There was a carriage house, river front that was promised to me. I wanted that for it seemed to fit my image of myself. However, that too was at a standstill. Suddenly everything that had been accelerated was now slowing to a crawl. I felt overwhelmed for I was not only planning a move and avidly packing; I was also going to doctors, massage therapy, etc. I became impatient. No matter what I did, nothing turned up. I found it hard trying to be in the present moment and to let go of any expectations. I wanted to move NOW!

Slowly events began to make sense in the standstill. I let go of moving and that felt right. I let go of any expectations with my lover realizing I couldn't make him love me, and besides, there was someone coming to me. I let go of my son and daughters. I even let go of my mother and my search for my sister. In essence, I let go of trying to make things happen in all areas of my life. I had finished writing the first draft of the book in two months. However, the editing was beckoning me. I wasn't able to heed its call. I was beginning to burn out. It was a time of letting things settle in order to sort things out.

I had quickly forgotten the Universal law of letting go. I had taken back my controls, and it wasn't working. I consulted a psychic and the gist was that my emotions were keeping me back. The shadow parts are right IN MY FACE. I don't want to be distracted or ignore them. So, the "half packed and ready to go" is one thing but now I have to do the work of housecleaning. What I didn't suspect, was the housecleaning was internally as well.

CHAPTER TWENTY-SIX: "HOUSECLEANING"

Housecleaning started Memorial Day when the insurance company terminated my massage therapy treatment. I became depressed, feeling abandoned, fragile and vulnerable. I felt like a boat with its moorings unearthed drifting out to sea in aimless direction. There was another part of me that felt free and accepting of this new stage.

I'm at the water's edge. The river is calm, the birds and ducks peaceful as well, and in turn, the peace permeated my being. There's so much letting go that I need this stability of nature. It's hard for me to stay still, however, when my peace is disturbed. The noise from thruway repairs at night forced me to seek refuge at a hotel two nights in a row at ll pm! I was seething with anger. My primitive nature was showing along with the seedlings and sprouts of letting go. I needed inner peace. It was as if there were two people inside of me warring with each other and neither wanted to give up the battle. I thought about my heart opening at the American Indian workshop this weekend. Perhaps it was letting go of the sadness.

Feeling more hopeful allowed new thoughts to enter, from a wholeness aspect. The effects of nature and quiet calmed me. Half packed and ready to go was indicative of both my state of mind as well as my pattern of life. Stay! Let go! Don't move! For letting go of the mother influence meant independence. But what would I do with that? The memories that have scarred my once whole and very tender heart kept me chained. The words kept on repeating insidiously in my mind. "Don't go! Don't grow! Don't leave ME!" Were they messages from the grave? Why was I half-packed? And didn't that occur previously when I wanted to buy an apartment across the street? "Make up your mind and the rest will follow," I thought to myself.

The inner conflict heightened - to be free, explore, see the world propelled me forward, while to stay put, as my parent's did, forced me back. One was my values; the other my internal parent. But which was my path? They were always there. Who am I there for? How do I reconcile the two? By having a sense that life is not either/or but a balance of many things and that I have free will. However, I questioned "How much free will do we really have?"

The time now is for me to dream, to have a vision of the future and be content in the present. "Be still and listen without judgment" was the message I had gotten in a meditation. I needed to heed that now. My mind was now made up. "I'm moving, half packed or not! And I'm moving into a more peaceful part of life, more effortless." That was my defined statement I needed to hear, as my heart heard it the other day. Sadness and confusion was beginning to be filled by quiet knowingness.

The combination of the Blessed Mother's presence in the Grotto, and recalling a psychic stating something about a Native American Ceremony, a pipe and a feather triggered many emotions. I felt it was another milestone; a marker of further progress. Certainly the opening of the heart, in such a dramatic way and setting, was evidence of movement.

One sleepless night of further frustration at not finding a new home, I received a message to pray. Pray I did. The next day I found an apartment in a nice neighborhood. I needed to make a decision about it within twenty four hours. Some things didn't feel right and so I sought out my realtor to ask if anything else had come in. There was another apartment.

We rushed to see it. It was as Madeline had said, "brick, tar, concrete," and only a mile away from where I lived on Rt. 9W! To make matters even better, it was an entire house, up on a mountaintop, just as I had wished for, with a magnificent view of the river and trees and nature all around. I had the space I dreamt about. Oddly enough it looked exactly like the home I had lived in with my family, right down to the striped wallpaper in the hallway. And another strange thing, the street name was the same as the one where the accident occurred. It felt right. I took it on the spot. Only there was one little thing that the realtor quickly mentioned. There's an apartment downstairs. A male nurse lives there but he's never home. I figured "one person, never home. Sounds good to me." Little did I know.

Cleaning out and housecleaning began, but it wasn't the kind I imagined. The day before I was to move in, I went to the house, so excited to bring my things there, to stake my claim. I got the shock of my life. There were people talking downstairs and the sounds were as clear as if they were right next to me. I wanted to run away for privacy and space were what I yearned for. However, I didn't act on my feelings. It cost me ten months of misery, financial loss and a re-connection to very primal emotions of rage. I was furious, but something told me the rage needed to come out.

My vision and intent around this move was that I'd have a quiet space to both entertain friends and edit my book. I recall another psychic saying that I needed to be very clear about why I was moving for it would be for a short time. I thought I knew the answer to both parts. But both were clouded for ten months by the "cave dwellers."

I soon found out that I was no longer in charge of my life, like it or not. I too was entering a cave, the abyss of negativity. I fought it vehemently. But to no avail. I was entering another cleansing period and I prayed that it would end soon. Oh how I prayed for that, but revisiting was upon me.

I couldn't stop the move at this point, for I was no longer in charge. The move in full swing, had every friend I knew help me with personal and fragile items, for the accident precluded my doing heavy work. My brother was both a big help and much support. The move went well. I put yesterday's event in the back of my mind, and bid "Good Riddance"to my love nest and now unbearable noisy apartment. When we left, my brother suggested I ask the Super if I could return, if need be. I was furious at his statement. I wanted nothing more to do with my former life, and former apartment.

I vividly recall what happened next. Once there, I began to conduct a ritual to cleanse my new home. I set up my incense and smudge sticks and began the ceremony. A few minutes later there was a note on my door stating that the nurse downstairs had breathing problems and would I insulate the door in the kitchen that led to their apartment? I took action and knocked on their door. That was to be the only time they answered. We joked about my "stinky incense." There was the nurse…and a wife…and a dog! And they were always home. Though we joked with each other, I felt uneasy about them. My gut didn't trust them and their "niceness." Time proved me correct. The woman was overweight. I knew full well her anger. I shared that and the connection wasn't healthy. We despised one another, though I had attempted to befriend her at first, I soon stopped, feeling I needed to be true to my feelings, the newly found feelings of rage!

My world had turned upside down. All the dreams I had, the goals I wanted to accomplish in this house came to naught. I couldn't believe the predicament I was in until I spoke to Madeline. She said that the noise externally was due to my internal noise. I was angry at her for that statement but I knew it was true. I needed to both cleanse and reorder my negative thoughts. It was also time to address my rage. This then is what led me to the "cave and it's dwellers."

Rant and rage I did. I'd come down to make my breakfast and they'd slam their doors. I felt as if I hadn't any privacy. I'd go out my front door and there was hardly any space for my car. There was no space for me, as in my childhood sleeping in the living room, as well as in my marriage. Where I had the dream of more space, I had less in paradoxically, a bigger area. I was back home in my former marriage, only without the real life characters, but ghosts of the past. These ghosts were more powerful, for they had brought me full circle to what I had fled from. "Why?" "Why," I thought and prayed. But "why" wasn't the right question. "What do I need to learn?" was more like it. It would take another move to find out.

The only good that came out of it was that I was away from the noise of the horrendous thruway! But I didn't entertain, I didn't finish my book. What I did instead was entertain those ghosts, to at last put them to rest. I also put to rest my fantasies of what, or who, I thought I was. I had to face my "beastie" side of myself as in "Lord Of The Flies." I was not a nice person those ten months for I had to fight, again, for MY SPACE.

Yet another cycle of packing prevailed soon after I moved in. I wanted out as quickly as possible. Another search began again to no avail. Conditions in the house worsened. People next door would fight as I had in my marriage. Each time that would occur paintings would fall off my wall, and I would crouch in fear as I heard them screaming and threatening one another. I was reliving my marriage. The last straw was when I discovered not one, not two, but five people living in "The Cave" with two dogs; one of which appeared at my front door and I was unable to go out. I called the police. Nothing came of it. The nurse again came to my front door indicating he thought I was crazy. Again the projections. I told him I was going to court to report the illegal apartment downstairs. He only laughed. Unbeknownst to me, they were planning to move.

And fight I did, winning and losing at the same time. I won my battle within myself but lost financially. I had retrieved my backbone, the same spinal backbone that was injured in the automobile accident that happened three years ago…the same injury that caused me to close my private practice…the same backbone that still hurt with its ageless pain, and tormented nights of sleepless fear, rage, confusion and frustration. My backbone caused me to stand up for myself, one last time, in yet another court battle. But how could I stand up to crooks? How could I stand up to the Cave Dwellers? I didn't have to. I chose not to stand up to crooks, but look for another place to live.

As to the Cave Dwellers, they showed their true colors; the colors I spotted the first day I moved in. They left like thieves in the night causing the landlord to "hold the bag" empty, from their not paying the rent. My purpose had been accomplished these ten months, ten horrific months. It was to cleanse that area as well for the illegalities ended with my stay. This much I know, there was a definite purpose for my going there and now my time had ended there as well.

And where did I wind up? The same apartment complex I had just left, only this time I had a view of my Hudson River. I ate humble pie, gladly. Fantasies were no longer necessary, for reality felt much better. I had given up my image of myself and retrieved my essence in it's place. The journey had ended. I had found myself, all parts of myself and now I was able to start the next part of my life for I had not only re-connected with myself, I had also re-constructed myself in a very different form. The necessary de-construction was now over. It was time for me to go on with the next part of my life…happily so, more humble, wiser than before.

CHAPTER TWENTY-SEVEN:
"LILACS, DEAD ROOTS AND ROSES"

I awakened to another Mother's Day without my children and much sadness. It was 9am, time to call Elide for we were planning to make a special day of it. I was groggy from sleep and lethargic from the night before, wondering how the day would go. Elide answered saying she also was tired. We spoke for a while and said we'd talk again at noon, in order to have a peaceful morning to putter around our respective apartments and come up with ideas on how to spend our day. I hung up. There were no calls from my children. It felt OK for I didn't want to hear a dutiful child, I wanted to hear a real child who was willing to talk about the issues. Better to have no call, than to have a forced call.

As I readied for the day, my thoughts went to the last chapter of the book; a body of work that I carried for such a stretch of time that I began to wonder whether it would ever be finished. How can I end the book? What wonderful insights can I leave my readers with? I had reread the final chapter and the more I did, the more I felt it didn't contain the essence of the book. In fact, I wondered if it contained my essence as well.

How would I describe the journey to wholeness from the "good little girl with white gloves and rosary beads to the cookie mother, dutiful wife, diligent student, social worker, therapist, Shaman, and finally to Goddess?" "How would I sum up my life till now?" Answers didn't come as I roamed around my newly found home so elegant, regal, peaceful, simple and comfortable. I didn't need to know right away. These tumultuous years have taught me that.

And will I ever find my sister? I've received two unsuccessful searches. The problem is that without a first name for her, they cannot go further, and I don't have that. So I psychically connect to her "Dear one, my search continues, waiting, hopeful, that there will be a resolution. How can it be otherwise; for your silent birth, and others, have been proclaimed along with mine, and my mother's! Till we meet again."

I thought of Mother's Day past and how different it is now. My mother was gone. I had spent mostly every one with her. That was not to be the case with my children. They were on their own, living in faraway places Where did I fit in? Thoughts of fitting in brought me suddenly back to the ten months of horror "on the mountain with the Cave Dwellers." I shuddered as I thought of it... mornings began with waiting to hear the final slam of doors banging announcing the wife's leaving, at which point I'd go downstairs to have breakfast... afternoons spent outside wherever the "nurse who was never home" wasn't...or raising my music louder than one of the other "Cave Dwellers" who remained, as to not hear their conversations or their barking dogs. Evenings were spent upstairs, quietly working on the book and hoping the next door neighbors wouldn't fight once they returned from work. "What a way to live," I thought.

How very different it was once I found my new home. I followed these reflections outside to my terrace with a cup of coffee in hand. My bird, Vita, now in his magnificent new white Taj Mahal cage, was happily singing. My silly little birdie! How I loved that little creature. Despite his diminutive size, his being provides me a with a great deal of pleasure from his presence, his joyful singing, and never ending acceptance of his caged fate. "He's probably the epitome of my inner joy that seldom emerges. At least, someone is carrying my eternal essence in some form or another."

The new home I prayed for, searched for, these past ten months, had been right "under my nose," so to speak. "This is really weird! I left the apartment, setting my sights on reachable yet lofty goals and now I'm back where I started from." Yet it felt right though the pieces to the puzzle didn't seem to quite fit...not yet, that is.

Once the court case regarding the "Cave Dwellers" was over, with no home in sight, I called the management of my former apartment complex. "Ginny, it's Elaine. I'm just wondering if you have anything in the front, on the top floor. Just inquiring." She heard the hesitation in my voice, said there was and would get back to me. Five minutes later the super called, wanting to know if I'd like to look at the apartment. Timing was right for I had been on my way there. It had been freshly painted, well lit, with a beautiful view of the river and the Tappan Zee Bridge. This time, I wanted to make sure that I wasn't making a mistake and asked if I could stay overnight. I slept on the floor, content within myself with the emerging, and surprising decision. It felt right and there wasn't any noise. Finally, I had my own space! I moved in a few weeks later.

I laugh now thinking of my lover's statement, once I decided on the move. "That's dumber than dog shit," says he. He was right, of sorts. Yet, who are we to question God's Plan? For once I agreed to follow the unchartered path, logic fell by the wayside, and experience took its rightful place.

The view of the Tappan Zee Bridge, as well as the Hudson River, is peaceful now. The river as smooth as a silent murmur. The trees outside are blowing wistfully in the spring breeze. My plants, now sunning themselves on the terrace, are responding to the congenial atmosphere here as well. "But what is this anxiety trying to tell me?" I knew part of it had to do with my Dad, now ninety four years old. And, of course, any routine medical check-ups leave me freaked out. But I believe it's related to another step; this time one in which I can't pinpoint the area in my life. Perhaps it pertains to a relationship change, my career or another spiritual encounter. Maybe all three!

It was time to meet Elide. She said she was going to wear a hat, which reminded me of the "hat fiasco" at Tracy and Chris' wedding. I laughed knowing that part seemed to be healed. I wore my red outfit that I designed and created, and a hat as well. We looked fantastic, sixty years old or not. We strolled along the river in my favorite place, Piermont. Though the town was packed with people honoring, in part, their mothers, we found a quiet spot at the water's edge in a small park. Quite naturally, our children, were the first topic. All live far away. Next, came our mothers, reminiscing about mine, as well as her mother whom she was going to visit in Switzerland. With her mother's failing health, her next task would be to try to convince her to accept assisted living. And, lastly, came our former husbands and lovers.

We laughed when the shrill fire whistle went off above our heads just as we were speaking about the men in our lives. "What was the message? What was the whistle blowing for besides the obvious reasons? Is there an alarm we needed to heed?" Or was this another relationship I needed to let go of? Perhaps, it was "just a cigar," as Freud would say. Denial swiftly moving into another battleground. I was intent on holding onto my lover, or was I? Is this the reason for my move to my "love nest?" Oh, another letting go? Not now, I'm not ready!" I put it in back of my mind. Surely, it will surface when the time is right. I prayed that it wasn't now.

The day slowly unfolded. Two beautiful and mature women, gracefully aging, sauntering along Life's and Piermont's promenades. Men and women, some happy, others not, peppering the sunlit day with their chatter. Stray male eyes darting a glance at us, we both oblivious to the stares, secure in our own beingness and lack of contrived behaviors. Hours passed, sunlight turned into sunset and we set about our next task...to retrieve, no, actually steal, lilacs from a favorite scouted out spot of mine - a corporate park.

On the way there the familiar mountain pass brought memories of my former home nearby. Elide asked if I wanted to pass by it in order to see how I'd feel, in order to see if anything else has to be healed. We planned to see what was going on there after the lilac caper. Actually, I had often thought about it, especially the couple next door, but hadn't acted on it. I thought about how much the house looked so like the home I had left from my marriage. It felt as if it were ages ago - lifetimes ago, yet all in one life. So much fullness has occurred since then. A fullness that ripened on Life's tree has given me such pleasure once pain was addressed and witnessed, in re-experiencing my past, now falling to the ground for the Earth's natural, comforting, and healing embrace.

Life was surely interesting and mysterious these days. First, I traveled to the mountaintop to enter the Cave dwelling, and now giggling like a school girl. The laughter was both freeing and passionate. I needed that to break the morning's tension. We arrived at the spot where the lilacs were. We were greeted by the quiet sounds of nature. The rotund and billowing bush was waiting for us. I hesitated at first, picking one or two in a surreptitious spot while my dear friend was gleefully attacking the bushes, retrieving huge bunches of flowers! I soon followed her outrageous behavior with my own. Here we were, elegantly dressed women, acting like children, and enjoying every minute of it!

Tears of joy come to my eyes, tears of sadness for my mother, her unborn children and my unknown and missing sister, still with whereabouts unknown according to my recent search. I hope wherever they are they're as happy as I am in this present moment of time and space. Interestingly, as I write this, there's a garbage truck across the street making a ruckus. Both the noise and my garbage do not grip me as before.

Next stop was the Cave. It looked forlorn. The young couple's apartment was empty. So that's why they were on my mind recently! They, too, had moved! My apartment was occupied and the kindly young girl downstairs next to the Cave Dwellers was still there with no one above her right now. She's probably enjoying the peace and quiet. There was a settled feeling in my body; no anger, regrets, or resentment just a peaceful sense of knowingness that my purpose there had been fulfilled and correct. The anger that I felt, had now changed to acceptance, compassion and forgiveness, for myself as well. I had moved on and been the catalyst for those who also needed the momentum to change as well. The purpose of the move, one that I knew the first day I entered the house, was now validated. I needed to revisit my marriage, one that I had left many years ago, but, nonetheless, still needing resolution.

"God, life is grand!" I thought, "Here I am, with Elide, a friend who has worked with me feverishly and devilishly to a truthful relationship that once was submerged, yet not suffused…and out of, and through, life's alchemical fires, we are unscathed from the heat, survivors, rising like the Phoenix out of ashes. Oh, how passionate I feel now about life, hope and love, and relationships. For now, I have a relationship with Self!

The final stop for Mother's Day was home, a home I looked forward to going to… a home that I entertained in…especially this weekend for my friend, Barbara, from the psych unit, came from California with her new fiance. And another friend unexpectedly called, and brought me roses for Mother's Day, and today with Elide. How different Life looks when one has found Hope.

We took a tour of my home looking, smelling, savoring the luscious roses, lilacs and orchids, almost as if they were our children. Once on the terrace, she spied my root bound asparagus plant, laughed, and said it needed to be trimmed. We discovered that the plant, housed in a piteous and almost discarded bathroom garbage pail was encased as well in its original pot! "This plant has given you such pleasure and look at the condition it was in."

Out came the butcher knife. Root upon root, rooted balls upon rooted balls, hanging inches deep, furthered our laughter. In fact, the height of the plant was equaled by the loftiness of the roots. The poor plant had not only survived, but thrived in its constricted environment!

Suddenly, everything in my life in the years since the car accident came full circle in an instantaneous flash! "My life was mirroring the plant!," I thought. Not only had I survived but I'm thriving as well. I hadn't taken care to put my loyal and loving plant in a more stately pot, I hadn't taken care of myself, either. Similar to my mother's bodily fate and my bodily fears. However, I can say that I'm living my life for probably the first time so totally in years.

With rejuvenated energy, and inflamed passion, I took hold of the knife freeing both the pot and myself cutting, digging, reaching, sawing, hurling clumps upon clump of ancient roots among the decaying dirt. There was a reverence about this ritual, so serendipitous, so unexpected this Mother's Day. "MY plant, the container of MY soul, abided and bore with me these many years; providing glorious and regal pleasures, with its spiraling, huge green tendrils that my eldest daughter admired. It came outdoors with me in spring and summer, by my bed in fall and winter.

This was the metaphor for my body, my body that I seldom cared for, yet it survives and thrives, despite myself. It has taken me lovingly on this journey to hope in relatively good shape. I was not only freeing the plant but claiming my essence and body at the same time, now united. The metaphor sparked in my mind the saying, "As so above, so below" seemed quite fitting now. Body and soul were now one as in Spirit and Matter. Another spark in my memory now knew why the word "embodied" had such a loaded impact on me when I wrote that in a progress note long ago. I knew that the anxiety message was indeed a joyful message. It was proclaiming new birth from new eyes, old tears and new experiences. My heart was full, no longer empty! My body indeed had taken me to a better place. My body had the answers!

And then the call from my eldest saying "I love you, Mom, and hurt when you're in pain…the eldest who left New York several years ago and left me in pain as well. This time she was saying "I Love You." Oh, what a gift time gave me. Then, and only then, was I able to take in the card from my grandchildren. Though not from my son, it told me he wanted some connection. And my youngest? The rest will come with new buds in a hopeful season and in God's time.

My life had come full circle, knowing that the de-construction and re-construction period is a portent of more to come. I had not only survived, I had changed my life and, in so doing, found myself in the ashes at the bottom of the pot, my shadow in bounded roots. They were the roots of the decaying past now allowing room for growth in a vision of hope and love. My journey now complete. I'm ready. To go. To grow. To not leave, but leap into the future.

The vision I had is now a reality…for there is not only one bird in my life but many surrounding me, multiplying and growing infinite with each day. I again go out on the balcony, the river is flowing endlessly on its course streaming, churning and never failing, getting to its rendezvous and destination only to come back again- to Life, from Death, to Life from Resurrection.

Thanks to you Mom. I have both the Love and Hope you lost long ago. Forgotten dreams are no longer hopeless nor are they forgotten…the journey to Love has reclaimed them. Sleep well, my dearest, your voice has been reclaimed. Rejoice in your many tomorrows! Happy Mother's Day!

CHAPTER TWENTY-EIGHT:
"THE BABY IN THE BUTTON BOX"

Writing this book took two months. Resolving the issue of finding my sister - a life time. "The book isn't finished." was what I heard from many sources. That was several years ago. I wondered what more could there be? Not knowing, or expecting what was to come, I set the book aside, as other things took precedence.

After a year of unexpected, mysterious happenings, a necessary update prompted looking into dormant, unanswered questions. A new chapter emerged as my life again transformed. It was March of 1999. Easter and Spring were just around the corner. I was in my usual morass, bogged down in another sluggish part of my life. I had my usual ambivalence towards the unknown; where mystery lies, along with creative gifts, but also fear and resistance. Sluggishness" is actually internal movement, silent, internal, productive. It is the boiler room movement that produces outer manifestations. Of course, when it occurs I never seem to remember the good, only the frustration.

While in that frame of mind, a website by the name of Lord Maitreya, spiritual in nature, called to me. I hadn't a clue to what the name signified. However, what was said resonated in my very being. I have since come to learn that Lord Maitreya is an Ascended Master, one who has been freed of the bounds of reincarnation, through achievement of mastery of one's material nature.

I compiled a series of informational packets on His teachings, and left them where they would be prominently seen; the local bakery, where many people gathered. I called it a "Lending Library." There were articles on the present phenomenal evolutionary processes that most citizens on Earth aren't aware of - I would venture to say, or even care about for we're all immersed in our ever increasing daily stressors. People were certainly reading the articles, for they disappeared. "Better to disappear, than not read at all,"I thought. The writings/teachings were so logical and intelligent, coming from this Ascended Master, that I wanted more. One day one of my questions was actually answered and posted on the site! A highlight of my seemingly dull life. I felt honored. The website included a personal touch with information on the New Zealand channel, named Margaret

Birkin. In time, I was informed that she was coming to New York City where she had spoken the year before at the United Nations, and would be available for private readings. The UN Society For Enlightenment & Transformation is a well respected organization I was familiar with, having attended numerous sessions. I sensed this was an opportunity that I would not let slip by. I immediately signed on for a personal reading.

Several months passed. I forgot about it, till one day Ms. Birkin phoned from NYC. We were soon to meet. I could hardly wait. I arrived an hour early, eagerly awaiting this new experience. I took the elevator up to the apartment after connecting with Ms. Birkin on the intercom. "Margaret", I thought. Of all names, that of my deceased mother. Did she have a hand in this, I wondered?" The elevator left me out on a narrow hallway. A door down the hall quickly opened and there she was. A huge, goddess of a woman, heavyset and proud of it, one could tell. Her husband was in the next room. He was tall and slim reminding me very much of my lover.

She introduced him and then escorted me into the next room for the session. I got a kick out of Margaret's humanness, as she was quite frustrated in struggling to make the tape recorder work. "Darn this thing. Let's have another go at it. It was working for the last person." After several tries, and prayers on my part, we were ready to go. "You're going to be a channel. You're going to have a very long life, and be very successful. You're just hanging on regarding your profession, not very satisfied, knowing something else is coming." It went on and on like this and felt right. I knew I had done the right thing. This is the "next step" I had been waiting for, knowing it would come, defending my position with family, friends and neighbors. I felt like a fool, and a failure. You name it, I felt it. But in the depth of my being, I knew it was right, no matter how crazy it seemed to others. Now, in that stranger's presence, I was hearing what I had longed to hear, but dared not hope or expect I ever would.

"You know it would be a good thing if you attended the group tonight, as well as my course down in North Carolina in a few weeks." A shiver went through me. I had known about what she was presenting, for in seeing the brochure the idea came to me that North Carolina was within driving distance. But as with this meeting, I put it out of my mind. Oftentimes, what was possible for others, seldom presented for myself. I pondered staying for the group meeting that evening, being ever careful of my money situation. However, money is never an issue when my intuition says otherwise.

The session at this point, brought up questions about a client that perturbed me as Margaret continued... "You were a powerful channel in a past life, but harmed people. However, it was due to manipulation on the part of another person." The connection was then made with the current client. It was she who had been the one that manipulated me in a past life! I was stunned, by that revelation, for there was something that felt unfinished with this person. I was overwhelmed at the power of past lives having such a dramatic effect on my current situation. The suddenness of change and challenges now presented to me, quickly summoned me to North Carolina and new beginnings.

I then knew it was important to attend the evening channeling group, which was well attended by mostly UN staff members. They were rather well dressed, intelligent "normal" looking people with a keen interest in what the mainstream may call "weird." I and they knew and most importantly, accepted it as a deepening layer of consciousness and connection with the Divine; a heightened form of spirituality.

Margaret channeled information from Lord Maitreya on global events, which were on the minds of all in the room, especially earth changes. It was fascinating to watch. She would begin quite consciously, in her own voice, till this "Ascended Master" entered. Her head would go to one side, drop like a lead ball down to her heaving chest, and out she was, in he came. Her voice deepened to a males at this point. I was familiar with this, having had experienced this off and on for the last several years, so I wasn't fearful of it. Peter was at her side, assisting with water for Lord Maitreya when His throat was parched. The energy coming from above is equal to thousand of volts, and so at some point, "The Master" needed replenishment in our Earthly density. The bantering that went on with the three of them was heartfelt. Lord Maitreya announced that most personal questions such as "What is my life's purpose" wouldn't be addressed. However, he would answer general ones that would apply to all. Not a pin dropped while he spoke.

A young girl sitting on the floor in front of me asked a question about when her time would come to channel. "Ask the woman in back of you how long she has waited." "That woman" was myself! I was stunned and pleased at the same time. Acknowledgment of my long suffering process gave validation. I told her "five years" when actually it was a lifetime, or lifetimes, waiting for my life's purpose. It FELT like many lifetimes rolled into one; the naive, Catholic young maiden, diligent school girl, secretary, young wife, mother of three beautiful children, and the long held twenty year dream of college, then grad school, finally becoming a therapist in private practice, and now awaiting the next phase of my life. I guess you would call it maturity! Only a maturity not in the usual sense of the word, but one that leads back to God.

I left there dazed and confronted with details, decisions to make regarding the trip to North Carolina. It didn't take as long as decisions usually do for me, and with my new car, gear packed, I spent the first part of my trip with my girls in Maryland and Washington, DC. They had not a clue where I was going. In fact, they acted as if I were going around the block instead of traveling hundreds of miles alone, starting out at 3:30AM on unknown, dark, foreboding roads.

There were protestors on the street corners, even at that hour, in downtown Georgetown, protesting the World Bank's position. It summoned my passion and I waved my support. I hesitantly followed the darkened, lonely road. Praying constantly the seemingly endless hours of the dark night. It seemed like an eternity till the dawn came, just like the saying. By now, I had calmed down. The pristine setting of giant pine trees and hardly anyone on the road felt as if the whole world had disappeared, leaving me with a wonderful, free feeling of space... all of it for myself, not having to share it with parents, husband, lover, children, clients, plants or my wonderful birdie. Just me, myself and I on the long road leading to the paradise once lost, and soon to be found.

I reveled in the freedom of beingness, with time to spare, time to explore. In between obsessing on where the next bathroom was (my only hindrance at my age), I passed rivers, streams, hawks flying overhead, deers grazing on the side of the highway, dew slowly evaporating from the morning's sunrise. First pit stop, a tiny roadside restaurant. Pickup trucks and families replaced the hustle and bustle of downtown Georgetown, or the suburban sprawl of Bethesda. Families emerged where there had been expressionless faces from whence I came. Perhaps they were coming from church, high on God, wanting ham and eggs and bacon instead of a skim double latte at Starbuck's. The smell lingered in my nostrils as I sped to the ladies room. The face in the mirror needed makeup so as not to shock myself or others. I stuck out like a red flag with my new Saab amidst the trucks, as well as being solo amidst the crowd and herd mentality. Sorry, that's the way I felt as a single person in amongst these couples and families. I quickly ordered a decaf coffee and left so as not to absorb the negative energy that goes with strangers in a tight knit community. The sun felt good as I sipped my coffee outside, amongst the roaring trucks quickly pulling in on the graveled road. "Time to go- too much crowd for me on a Sunday morning!"

Another pit stop afforded me a look at a college town, now more nattily dressed, in couples, but not families as much, venturing into a supermarket amongst the profusion of colors of Spring flowers, newly emerging from the winter frost, sleet and snow, peeking their hesitant buds anew at the many faces of emotion on passerbys. I liked the feel of this town, mindful of the unnecessary need of comparison. Nary a bump in the road, no potholes, no traffic signs littering the highway more profusely than actual debris. The towns faded into country roads with horses, cows and tiny ponds spewing forth vapors of early morn flowing upward to be blessed by morning sunlight. This was heaven, nothingness, nirvana. But reality called to venture further.

Sensing the nearness of my new adventure, not knowing exactly where it was, I stopped at a gas station, which sold baked goods, fresh from the farm, amongst the residue of day old cigarette butts strewn on the street. Just like life. This was the first time I asked for directions, and was closer than I thought. Just like life. I went "up the road apiece" and there on the corner was a giant barn housing, of all things, a manufacturing plant. What a disappointment to travel to the countryside and find such a site. Acceptance set in, yet again, and I continued on the rural road, around the corner, up the bend and found two horses greeting me from inside a fenced in area. I waved "Hello" as if they were neighbors, and continued onward, eager to find the retreat house. Birds were singing. Other than that, nary a noise of the world, but those of nature. Another long, pebbled driveway and I was at Sacred Grove!

As I pulled into the driveway, there was Peter on the veranda. Has my lover followed me here in Peter's form, I thought? "Hello, Elaine, we've been waiting for you" said Peter, in his shy, somewhat hesitant, but cordial manner. Alongside him were strangers who would soon be friends. My mystical side was about to "spring a leak" and the watershed would be the Great Dividing line between believers, non-believers, inside and out of my closest relationships.

In the trunk was packed a metaphor of my indecisiveness about things mystical, which seem to always get me into trouble or pain. Notwithstanding those negativities, the upside was the road at the end of the road less traveled, and I was about to find something in that trunk that was to bear fruit...for my coming out party was in the dormant stages. In driving home, I was told "You have not yet arrived!" That put me in my place!

Amidst the many clothes I had packed, was a lavender colored finely knit, exquisite handmade velour shawl. My daughter, Lisa, and I had been furniture shopping in a swanky shop in downtown Bethesda. As I passed a bedroom set I spied this shawl lying atop the bedding. It called to me as night to day. I heeded the call, went over and lovingly picked it up, as if caressing a lover's body. It felt smooth to the touch. The shawl was soft and beckoning. I couldn't put it down, try as I may. The conflict of "should I or shouldn't I" began and didn't end until I pulled up to the driveway in North Carolina. "What do I need this shawl for? After all, I would feel guilty because Mom made me so many Afghans? I really can't afford it. It's too expensive?" And on and on and on, disgusting myself, all the way here. Finally, I simply had to make a decision for Lisa wanted to leave. "That's it! I'm getting it!" said I, defiantly. Out came the well worn Visa card and I gulped as I paid for it, carrying like a newborn to the trunk of the car, where it stayed two days, along with the conflict of pleasure vs practicality. There it stayed in the trunk, where almost every minute of the travel time spent was taken up with the ever pressing decision. But enough of my crazies.

I got out of the car and viewed the surroundings. The house was in better shape than I thought, for my conversations on the phone with the proprietor, Marilyn, indicated that the only running water was in the main house. With New York mentality, I imagined a back road environment. So much for my negativity. It was a lovely huge, log cabin with porch, swing, rocking chair and a three-legged dog (thanks to the rednecks in the area that didn't like things unknown such as a retreat). There was a flower garden with my favorite irises in them, along with hummingbirds darting to and fro. In the far distance I could see a neat looking trailer, the one I would have gotten if it had running water! And the loveliest looking people on the porch all staring at me, yet another stranger to these parts.

Marilyn was recently widowed. A slim, attractive woman in her 40's comfortably dressed. Marilyn was the reason...well, I'm not going to reveal that right now. You'll just have to wait a bit, like I did! Marilyn and her deceased husband Karl are musicians. Karl a composer. Marilyn a harpist. They decided before he died that their home be turned into a place of rest and renewal - a spiritual retreat center. Lise came from Brooklyn, who later turned out to be a true friend and colleague of mine. There was Karen from LA, a talented writer, humorist with a haunting past. There was Jeannie, a widowed massage therapist, and a Southern Belle, teacher at a nearby college, as well as one male in the group. We had one thing in common, a shared interest; that of learning about the mysterious ways of the world. We were there for four days, a small time to render after waiting a life span for what was mine in a past life.

People, food, merriment, dogs and cats and music abounded that and every day hence. We immediately gathered in the large, comfy living room, a concert harp stood in front of a stained glass window, regal and quiet for now. The gentle breeze outside stirred the rich sounds of a wind chime. Cat and dog constantly roamed freely in and out of the revolving animal opening at the bottom of a screened doorway. There was a fireplace adorned with pictures of the family. Marilyn had two children; a married daughter, an artist whose room I shared with the computer, and Mark, a music teacher at a nearby college, well versed in the mystic and about to embark on a new horizon along with his mother.

We began after lunch. Peter stayed quietly busy in the nearby kitchen as Margaret set up shop. She was all business. I liked that. She took charge, started and ended the, (what shall I call them), meetings? on time. Well, they weren't really meetings in the sense of just people on earth coming together, you see. Meetings in the sense of meeting with Spirit, you see, or don't or can't or won't see. I took a seat near the window and door, with full view of inner and outer. Margaret began. "We're here to learn about Spirit. The first lesson I can tell you is to just surrender, and all else will flow." Notebook to the ready, pen in hand, I started my school girl note taking in shorthand which freaks everyone out 'cause they can't understand a word, errr, scribble, on the blank page. Since my lack of controls were limited, I reveled in this. One by one, unannounced, we began to 'zone' out. I saw Marilyn's eyes close, and bingo, she was a goner, head tilted back, looking as if she were intently listening to one I knew not. Margaret tended to her flock lovingly, knowing full well what was happening and explaining it to those who needed explanations.

I felt a sense of calm, at ease in these environs as much as others fear. My crown chakra began 'whizzing' and I knew something or someone was about to give me a message. I sunk more deeply into my chair, awaiting the unknown. At times there would be conscious messages; at others just the process of energy surging through my body. Either way it was information, whether I understood it or not. I surmised for use when I needed it, much like a packed sandwich for noontime lunch. These processes were the order of the day for the four days.

Dinnertime soon came. A much needed break. It was early afternoon. I needed to be alone, while others went about chatting with each other. I went to my car, my temporary and secure home base. Wanting to get something from the trunk, I opened it and was startled by hearing an inner voice say "Take in the shawl. See if anyone wants to buy it." Red lights flashed. Bells, whistles and sirens went off. Bingo. A hit. My sense of shame at asking if someone, strangers no less, wanted to buy the velour shawl. I shut the trunk down faster than when I opened it, figuring a slam would rid myself of the inner and instantaneous turmoil. It didn't work. I sat in the front seat, floundering around my pocketbook for some gum, something I know I do when I get tense. Ah, a lifeline to save me from myself! Didn't work this time. I reopened the trunk. Yup, the shawl was still there, awaiting extradition to another home. Was I ready to let it go? After all, the internal conflict hadn't been resolved.

Jeannie was the first shawl encounter. Jeannie was a massage therapist from around the area who wanted to be a friend. I shied way as I prefer to be alone, as this place wasn't what I was used to. There was hardly a site to isolate myself, except my car. "Jeannie, I've got this shawl I bought in Maryland. Decided not to keep it (a sort of lie at that point). Want to buy it?" The silence was as deafening as my shame. I felt total rejection. Afterwards, she told me she got a message not to say a word!

Head bowed, I slowly entered the kitchen. "Damn Spirit. I don't want to do this." Silently, I knew I had to, should do, ought to. Whatever! Marilyn was at the sink, deep in work and thought. My anxiety level was off the charts. "Er, Marilyn...holding up the shawl, I'm returning this shawl I bought in Maryland. Do you think you'd be interested in buying it?" Just say it Elaine. Get it over and out. "Are you sure you want to part with it?" Am I sure? Am I sure? No. Yes. I don't know! "Yes, I'm sure." "How much is it?" "Ninety Dollars?" Silence. Pause. "Oh, I don't know, it's a lot of money." Silence on my part. Pause. "Marilyn, I have a sense you deny yourself things. Is that correct?" Bingo. I hit the jackpot. "You're right, Elaine. Let me try it on." She goes upstairs with something on her mind and comes down clothed in a lavender dress the exact color of the shawl! "It's mine!" She proudly exclaims, as I had several days back. I got this dress for a bargain, and look, it is exactly the same color." Others come into the room. We all "ooohd" and "aaahd". The buzzing on top of my head is louder now. I know something is in the works, but still I have to wait. I had a sneaking suspicion she needed to have the shawl, not me.

The afternoon session begun, money in my hands, shawl on Marilyn's shoulders. She looked like a Goddess in it and proudly showed it off. I felt good about what I had finally done! We begin. Margaret is silent. Lord Maitreya, the "guy" who started it all comes through. Actually, Lord Maitreya is an Ascended Master, like Jesus, Mary and Buddha. People usually look askance, thinking "What the hell does that mean?" I inform them of the above, as I was. People need that fact. I did. Well, to get back to the present, or should I say, the future soon to be here, Margaret "zones" out, Lord Maitreya "connects," and with a loud, booming voice says "Elaine". I freeze. What now?

"Elaine, you were in a great deal of conflict in what we in Spirit arranged as a present for Marilyn. When you were in doubt, we were in knots, saying 'Oh, what'll we do now.' For you see, we go to a great deal of trouble to line things up for what you humans call "synchronicity" and if the opportunity is lost, we have to start all over again. We do not get angry. However, we do get disappointed. So we were very happy when you heeded your intuition, finally!" "Not going to do that thing, again, I thought!" I learned my lesson. Did I?

All eyes on me. Of course, I had to have a word in "But, Lord Maitreya, I did it!"We all laughed. Lesson learned, for all of us. All eyes were on me again towards the end of the workshop when Lord Maitreya again singled me out saying I had a hard life, and my rewards would be in Heaven. I was angry and responded. "What about here?" No answer, only that I am at some point to move to Florida. Oh, my. Here we go again!

One of the most significant turning points were when I was infused with Spirit. I was filled with a feeling of love so powerful, I had to get up and exclaim, proclaim it. At one point, I laughed when I received the words "Shut up, and just stand there." I couldn't do otherwise as even an attempt to take a tiny step, in my arrogance, failed. I could not move. Finally, I gave up and just lay down filled with pouring, surging energy of Love! A love so pure, a love so genuine, that made me weep. Margaret assured my newly found friends I'd be OK and I was more than OK at the end.

The other phenomenal experience I had was when Margaret was channeling about past lives. I really didn't give much thought to past lives, for I had all to do to handle this one! I had my rings on. My lovely engagement ring on my right hand that Lisa recently admired. I said it would be hers one day. On my pinky finger of my left hand was a wedding band bought after twenty five years, naively meant to be a symbol of a remarriage ceremony, without asking my husband about it! Oh, my, was I ever unconscious those days. The wedding band was magnificent, with sparkling baguettes in a gold setting. I hardly ever wore them unless I went to a social setting where there were couples. The rings were my escort into the couple world where I once had been.

In any event, I was zoning out as Margaret spoke and heard the words "Give your ring to Lisa. Buy yourself another one! Go upstairs and see Peter." I surmised that I needed a past life reading and heeded Spirit's promptings. But I was summarily disappointed! Peter was speaking with The Master and couldn't see me! Down the stairs I go. Now Margaret is talking about resolutions of an old marriage. I begin to cry. I knew the rings meant the end of a marriage that divorced me from my husband and children fourteen years ago! Old tears. Oh, my, so old! I now connected Peter with my lover and knew then that was over as well. Or was it? I had gotten my gifts of prophecy and of letting go's. I had done good, as my lover would say. I felt secure about my intuitive urges to come and follow Spirit in the oddness and newness of this experience. I wasn't expecting what would come once I left North Carolina.

Towards the end of our stay, I was handed a letter by Marilyn, which would put me in touch with a mentor, and trusted friend in this and a past life. It was from a fellow harpist in Connecticut. I read it and wept. So beautifully written, filled with passion and love for life, that I was moved to contact him. "That person" turned out to be a Pharaoh in a past life.

No sooner did I leave North Carolina that my challenges started! Silent whisperings began. You could call them intuition, sensing, knowing, thoughts, visions. Whatever. They were stronger now than ever before. "Go visit Uncle Pete on the way home." "Well, that makes two of us, for I thought it as well." My mother's brother was dying of lung cancer. I was told I'd win the lottery and given specific instructions concerned my children and the alleged winnings. This was the first lesson in surrender, ridicule and confusion regarding Spirit's ways. Which are not that custom on Earth! In any event, I was certainly a different person in a very short period of time. My head was spinning, not from energy, but from the new hat I willingly had put on. But that was nothing compared to those who came in contact with me.

I stayed with Lisa on the way back after going through the Blue Ridge Mountains. It was a wonderful journey, in ways, back in time when my husband and I went to Monticello and Charlottesville, VA, ostensibly to "celebrate" our twenty-five years together. Instead, all we did was fight. It was a miserable vacation, as I thought traveling the magnificent highway. I stopped along the road to fetch loose rocks for my altar. I stopped alongside a beckoning bench and a waterfall. I drove to Jefferson's home but it was the week before Easter and jammed with tourists. I proceeded to my refuge in nature. I didn't want the winding road to end.

However, it had to. I was now in the Washington area happy to see family. I stayed with Lisa. Strange messages and tests had unknowingly began. I received a vision of a gas station in NJ and told to buy Lottery tickets for my entire family there. I did as I was told, much to the consternation of my family. "Disconnection" had begun. I felt sure I was going to win. But putting it aside, I visited my other daughter, Tracy, her husband Chris, and wonderful grandson, Matthew. His face emulated the purity of love I felt in North Carolina, which was soon becoming a fading memory, but not of experiences heart and body felt. The visit was bittersweet as I needed to leave them behind. Nary a question was asked of my trip. Rings freely given to daughters gave me a sense of closure. Backing out of their driveway, I waved Goodbye for what felt like a lifetime till I saw them again.

On the way home, I thought of Uncle Pete and intended to visit him. We weren't on the best of terms since my mother died and I told family members about the suspected sister. However, he was ever loving to me, but I didn't quite feel that way, yet. The drive took longer than expected and I was tired. However, there was one thing that kept me going. The Lottery tickets. I felt it was a sign. Indeed I was told to buy lottery tickets there for the entire family. The hour was late. I had my newest conflict. What do I do, go to the gas station, buy the lottery tickets or visit my uncle?

The conflict was resolved when I found myself panicking for I was on the wrong highway for the intended winnings, surely, of the lottery tickets I was told to purchase! In fact, I found myself on the road headed to Uncle Pete's house! How very convenient of Spirit to get me off the track, wrong or right, to where I needed to go. Obsessing about the gas station, or where to buy the lottery tickets, I tried to call his house. No answer. Anxiety ridden I followed my newly used instincts to his home.

I rang the bell. He answered as if he was expecting me. He was. "Uncle Pete, I came here because I was told to. Do you know who told me?" Nonchalantly he calmly said: "God!" Well, I guess we're on the same wavelength, this time! Ray was there as well. He was

Uncle Pete's and Aunt Carrie's nephew. We sat down. I told them my hunch. They couldn't help me. I tried to let it go. But how could one let go of the idea of winning the lottery compared to visiting a dying relative! You can see where my priorities were, certainly not spiritual in nature, but very earth, ego, desire bound. In any event, we were having a wonderful time when the buzzing on my head started. "Uncle Pete, there's a message coming in. Do you want to hear it?" He and Ray said "Yes" and the first "coming out" channeling started...Uncle Pete's eyes were closed, Ray's intently focused on me. I closed mine, said a prayer and waited. "You are surrounded by Angels, Uncle Pete...above, alongside and always there with you. Have no fear. You are protected, loved and cared for." The messages stopped. I began to cry. I knew why. Deceased ones like his wife, my Aunt Carrie, my mother, Margaret, Aunt Florence, Uncle Paul, Uncle Bill were there." My sobbing intensified. Silence filled the spaces where fear had been. Uncle looked calm, as did Ray, as I peeked at them. There were no more messages. My mission had been fulfilled...my uncle need to hear the message of love from Spirit.

It was time to go. We said our now more deepened heartfelt Goodbye's and I raced to the gas station, only to have the lights go out as I got to the door. Desperation led me to knock on it. A quiet Indian gentleman let me and another hope filled gambler in. I bought tickets for my family and felt filled up with love in my heart. Again, I did not heed my intuition until it caused me grief. When am I going to learn my lesson, I thought. Soon enough as the lessons grew ever more frightening.

I didn't win the lottery. I was terribly disappointed and confused. I now was learning the ways of Spirit big time. Surrender Elaine. Surrender. Uncle Pete recently died a year later; the summer of 2000. The funeral was filled with so much love and surprise messages from beyond the veil. As I approached the casket, knelt down to pray, I heard "Elaine, I am so sorry. I now understand what you are doing for the family. I promise to help you." Uncle Pete was now speaking to me from beyond the grave. Knowing full well the ridicule and scorn, but having the strong sense that it may do some good, I told his son, Bob. Bob was in a great deal of pain, and anything that would alleviate it was welcomed, as were these messages of love.

Pete and I were at peace with one another. We had many e-mail communications before he passed on, mostly healing, filled with love, understanding, forgiveness, but not acceptance until he died. Uncle Pete felt I was "too religious" and "needed to get on with my life, leave the past behind." What if getting on with my life meant revisiting the past one last time in order to find and understand something that was an integral part of moving on? I felt in my heart that my life's journey, as well as past lives, meant for me to reconnect with something or someone I knew not which.

That I had a sister was a fact, not a supposition. Things said, unsaid pointed to that. However, I was unprepared for another fact. That I have a brother as well! I didn't have to seek it out. It all came to me one fateful day. I had received an upsetting e-mail from my uncle before a visit to my father. I wearily journeyed the familiar, well-worn path to the Bronx. Towards the end of our visit, he insisted I take my mother's button box, an old fashioned, black enamel box with bright red roses imprinted on the lid. "You never know when you'll need a button. It seems like a waste to throw them out." "It was also a waste to throw out my doll house, my Sonja Henie figure skating doll, and the wheels and handlebar of my children's beautiful navy and white English baby carriage, the "Cadillac" of all coaches!" I had tearfully retrieved the forlorn body (the carriage's or mine?) before my father had his way of letting go, and throwing it away. I brought it to my husband's home to keep. It is still there, the ghost of the past, a testimony to our once beautiful, whole family.

Of course I couldn't remind father of his thoughtlessness, only he could of others and I keep silent. Reluctantly, not wanting to have yet another heated "discussion," I took the box. I was still hurting on the way home from my uncle's remarks, piled now with further burden from my father's visit. I returned to my home, my quiet haven from all the thunder. I ignored the contents as I had for several months now, subconsciously not wanting to revisit the past my uncle had spoken about, but drawn to. The desire, however, had its resistence until that night.

Weary, yet unable to sleep, I opened the box slowly off its' rusty, noisily aching hinges. Inside was piled high with buttons from eons ago; sweaters Mom had knitted, clothes long gone the way of threadbare garments. The buttons peered up at me with many eyes, as if to say "What are you looking for inside our halls?" After displacing the myriad looking buttons, I spied something, an unfamiliar shape. It was the size of a thumbnail in width and length, blue in color; the tiniest of containers lying proudly, seemingly long hidden beneath old memories of worn out clothing.

The archetypal symbol of a most meaningful memory - of another child long ago given away, shorn from his mother's breast, as the buttons were from the barely connecting threads of new, then old, tattered, discarded garments. There in his lonely and somewhat cherished and comforting hiding place, was my brother, encased in a tiny oval frame. His cheerful, darling smiling face peering sideways at the viewer, dressed in a navy blue sailor suit. He looked like a happy fella, around 12 - 18 months old, sandy hair, adorable wide wonder-filled eyes that made me cry. Tucked inside this hollow yet hallowed container was a miniature Miraculous Medal, blue in color. I conjured up an image of my mother, saddened to the marrow of her bones, lovingly and tenderly placing it near her lost son; placed there by his mother, and my mother. I acted swiftly, partly due to revenge by having the tiny photo put on a disc and e-mailed to my relatives. I wanted them to know full well my mother's silent pain, and that the "fruit of her womb" did not go unnoticed or unclaimed by our family heritage. I also wanted some one to share my heavy burden for I was overwhelmed at another loss, another "what if" or "what could have been."

Shock, disbelief but with a certain acknowledgment "Who is the father?" was my uncle's response. Yet another dictum to "get on with life" and "would you want to write that about your daughters?" In essence, he was trying to shut me up. I would not budge. Other members nary a peep, much less a word of, or reply to, the truth of the matter. Again, I am left alone to share a secret, along with the burden - in deep connection with another mother - mine.

This "mother" burden continues to this day with my children, as well, for I have finally come to a place of putting behind the past; first through anger and action at those who have hurt me the most, my children and my father. I've set strict boundaries and "divorced" my children. In fact, they have "divorced" me sixteen years ago when I left their father. The unsettling fact is that I've never been forgiven for that. I put it out there, as I had when I found out about my sister and brother. No one wishes to listen. Now this wrenching letting go process is timely.

It is necessary to start yet again. The prompting of my heart call to me. The need to let go was now externalized in integrating the many copies of this, as yet, unpublished book that was begun with a request for a miracle from the Virgin. This is the closure, long coming and much misunderstood by myself and my family, that is necessary to finally "bury" the past, in order to sing in the present, and to dance in the future. Oh, it is so terribly wrenching and hard!

Again, it is I that starts the digging. It is I that unearths the memories. It is I that has the passion to overcome the denial. It is I that wants closure for the hurt, the undeniable hurt it has wreaked on our family that has to be ended. My recent gifts of channeling, communicating with the deceased, even becoming the deceased, as well as energy healing from Ascended Masters, have been my focal point this and last year. I had found my life's purpose, and as with everything else in my family, it is unacceptable! Sleepless nights, no communication with daughters, son. Control issues now rearing their ugly head with grandchildren. Enough! Enough! No more, I cry out. The deafening silence hits me like a brick wall.

I vow to put my energy into integrating the book; for in doing so I am integrating a piece of myself as well. Time has pulled me away from it, busy with yet another gift, that of channeling God's healing energies to self and other. This recent "gift" has taken me down a new and lonely road, devoid of road maps of religiosity, ritual, or the sacred or profane. Pertaining to the deepening spirituality calling me, magnetizing me with the energy from above, opening my heart to more compassion, but first a compassion to myself. I am determined to be true to my self. It can only help with others. Yesterday, as I was driving, I spied a license plate "True2one." Yes, true to One, and the Oneness of all. True to essence isn't always accepted by others, I have found.

Recent days were spent wandering after a most glorious nine months of living anew in Life's recent mysterious and unexpected gifts. Certainly, ones that I had long ago contracted before I was born, that I am sure of. It has taken me a lifetime to reclaim, to rediscover, to remember my very essence, my very being, my very passionate purpose in this lifetime. Therefore, the news of a brother,

149

and a sister were yet another ticket to put in a slot yet unclaimed, and unopened. There were no keys to enter, yet today felt different for I awakened early, which was a sure sign that internal work was now manifesting in a new birth.

I sought answers this morning from God, my guides, my angels, and especially my deceased mother, gone five years physically, but not consciously. I felt my crown chakra pounding with energy as I sought answers. Focusing on the presence of the Almighty, the Divine, silencing the ongoing mind chatter, I asked and I received. "I wish to contact my Mother, divine One/Beings. I wish to know what to do about seeking my siblings. Does my Mother, and Spirit, want that?" My ever strengthening communion and knowing of the Oneness with us all, and the certainty that we are all One, caused me to phrase the question in that manner. I am no longer alone. I know that I am cared for by others, somewhere "up there" or "out there" or "above". I know that they are with me right now for again the energy is pouring through the top of my head, for that is the spiritual connection, as real as plugging into a computer, or a phone line as you will ever know.

I had deep intent this time. Usually, I find that I may ask a question half-heartedly, and then suddenly not wanting to hear the answer, I conjure up distraction after distraction. This time there were none. I opened to silence, awaiting, suspended, but not expecting, any controlled answer. I surrendered to what is, to the truth.

The answer came. I opened my heart tentatively, wincing internally with the words that were to come, not coated in sugar pills, but pure truth. I waited. My breathing in and out the only tool I could use right now to find the answers. And then "Mother does not want any disturbance of their lives. Go on with your life." Tears come and came to my eyes, then and now. I thought "so in keeping with my mother. Don't upset the apple cart. Keep silent!"

Acceptance comes with more pain. It is truly difficult to accept "what is" rather than "what could or should be." I dusted off the pages of my manuscript, careful to not let the tears stain the pages that contained my love effort of ten years! I had found the answer to "What is Love?" Love Is, it just Is.

FOR NOW A "GOODBYE" - UNTIL WE MEET AGAIN

As a testimony, to lineage, unconscious connections and generations past, I mention the following:

Several years ago, I found myself walking on a path at a nearby hospital on my way to a doctor's office, for an examination related to my accident. I didn't consciously notice what was at my feet as I was deep in thought. However, on my return after the visit, I began to take notice of names and dates.

I soon realized that it related to infants that had prematurely died. Each were engraved in tiny and numerous stones on the path. I said a prayer for each of them. On the way home, I felt it odd that I noted that. Later that same day, my daughter was undergoing the trauma of losing her very first child to a miscarriage. In some way, I had been connected to my child as she to hers in that sad moment in time.

The following is a dedication to all the babies that have been lost, and continue to be mourned for in my family. They are all a part of us, and we rejoice in their presence. They are not forgotten.

Elaine Cordani-Gelhaus

MEMORAE

For a brief moment, an angel was sent to you,
And a tiny baby was formed in your womb.
Connected to your gentle, sweet body,
With its heart and soul.

And then in a swift moment in time,
She, or he, was gone!
But the memory of what was -
and what could have been lingers on.

It is to this memory that we give praise, and thanks and glory!
For theirs and your mission was not in vain.
We shall remember your memory - Through Eternity.
We love you. We wanted you. We cherish you.
and we thank you for your gift.
Go in peace, sweet children - Till we meet again.

THE BABY IN THE BUTTON BOX

"The Picchioni Family" Father, Severino Stepmother - Rose

Children:

From <u>right to left:</u>- My mother, Marguerite, William, Florence, Peter and Paul

SONNET CXVI

Let me not to the marriage of true minds
Admit impediments. Love is not love
Which alters when it alteration finds,
Or bends with the remover to remove:

O no! It is an ever-fixed mark
That looks on tempests and is never shaken;
It is the star to every wandering bark,
Whose worth's unknown, although his height be taken.

Love's not Time's fool, though rosy lips and cheeks
Within his bending sickle's compass come:

Love alters not with his brief hours and weeks,
But bears it out even to the edge of doom.
If this be error and upon me proved,
I never writ, nor no man ever loved.

William Shakespeare (1564 - 1616)

About the Author

I am a psychotherapist, baptized in, and early on devoted to my Catholic faith, but through mind and bodywork experience, moved into realms of deeply intuitive and psychic phenomena of tremendous mystical and shamanic proportions, having been mysteriously visited by, and trained with, a Shaman, a Himalayan Swami and a Pharaoh, who informed me that in our past lives together, I was Queen Hatshepsut in Egypt. All suddenly came at a critical junctures in my spiritual development, similar to my deceased mother's visit from the otherworld.

First and foremost, I'm a mystic called "a fire dancer by Spirit." I've had a myriad of experiences in a realm many scoff at, judge and persecute, but few follow. It meant venturing off the beaten path and facing challenges head-on through the alchemical fire of purification. At times, my skin and my body have been metaphorically burned beyond recognition by Life's fires of ignorance, persecution and negative human emotions. It has been a hard road, but I wouldn't have it any other way. For this was my contract with God before I was born. Coming to acceptance, however, took a lifetime.

Life's painful passion has steered my soul journey from current to past lives and back again, garnering relationships seemingly from this life, but really ones of the past, calling for healing, with self or another, or both. Before I married at twenty-one, I sought an answer to "What is Love?" Though I asked a parish priest, family doctor, and finally a psychologist, my inquiry went unanswered. Close, yet often tumultuous relationship with parents, especially with my mother's many illnesses, led the journey. My questioning love was the thread that intermingled with her lost hope from life's painful traumas that formed the exquisite tapestry of life's purpose.

Silently and insidiously, love led my soul yearnings and became my life purpose. I counsel clients on their soul's journey, guiding them into ever deepening, and much misunderstood world of God's wonders – though thoroughly documented in Eastern and Western sacred scriptures, and scientific research in altered states of consciousness.

Pain was the symptom, passion the energy – to reclaim parts of self through work on the psyche, as well as my human energy field through bodywork. The road took a sudden turn when my deceased mother appeared to me, while receiving bodywork, asking me to write about her life and informing me that I have a sister whom I never met, living in New Jersey – the result of which is the creative process of this book.

My trust, wonder and awe of God's mysterious Universe enabled me to come to Essence, for the soul is relentless in pursuit of excellence. Whether

I liked it or not, I was forever prodded onward to healing. I became a Transformer of Spiritual Energy, as in my past lives. Through the journey of the past and present, I have come full circle again.

My journey started with one question; with answers and experiences that continue to surpass my wildest dreams. Unbeknownst to me, my questioning love was the thread intermingled with my mother's lost hope from life's painful traumas, that forged a connections with four generations of Italian American ancestry, and formed an exquisite tapestry of my life's purpose.